D1500659

Dysfunctional Practices

that Kill Your Safety Culture
(and what do to about them)

Timothy D. Ludwig, Ph.D.
Safety-Doc.com

ISBN: 978-0-9998616-1-5

Calloway Publishing
Blowing Rock, NC 28601

Editor: David Johnson

Cover Art: Bryan Jurus

Book Design: Gretchen Kriesen

For Lori

Contents

Forewords

I DID NOT REALIZE THE VARIOUS DISADVANTAGES of using labels and other mental short-cuts (e.g., fishing for faults, blaming the victim, etc.) until reading, *Dysfunctional Practices*. This is but one lesson in this "page turner" in which Tim Ludwig describes re-search-based principles of human dynamics so you can relate to them, understand them, and apply them. You'll grasp how these principles of psychological science explain realistic life events in the workplace–often dysfunctions–and you'll realize how to correct them to develop effective injury-prevention interventions.

Tim's book offers a most memorable and invaluable learning expe-rience. In *Dysfunctional Practices* you will learn practical solutions to time-worn safety dysfunctions that will enable you to help achieve and sustain a work culture of people routinely actively caring for the health, safety, and wellbeing of others.

Timothy D. Ludwig is one of my former Ph.D. students. Teachers are reinforced whenever they note a former student making a positive difference. My positive reinforcers: Tim is a decorated teacher as a Distinguished Graduate Faculty at Appalachian State University. He is a highly respected researcher with scholarly books and dozens of research articles to his credit. He is a successful consultant with clients all over the world. His keynote speeches are the rave at professional conferences. And his work with the non-profit Cambridge Center for

Behavioral Studies (CCBS) delivers on their mission to apply behavioral science to benefit humanity.

I can see lessons I've been teaching throughout his book. Those critical lessons and even phrases are now being passed on to a next generation of readers. Moreover, this leading-edge book is even more reinforcing for me because of the new ground Tim has cultivated by integrating his own profound knowledge--gained through teaching and real-world consulting--into an ingenious presentation of safety-related dysfunctional practices, why they occur, and how to correct them.

"We live, we love, we learn, and we leave a legacy." This profound quotation from Stephen R. Covey, author of The Seven Habits of Highly Effective People, has fueled my motivation to keep teaching university students at Virginia Tech. I am empowered by this remarkable teaching/learning legacy. Once I was Tim's mentor and he my student; with this this book the roles are reversed. In many ways my former student has become my teacher.

E. Scott Geller, Ph.D.
Alumni Distinguished Professor, Virginia Tech
Senior Partner, Safety Performance Solutions

DYSFUNCTIONAL PRACTICES IS ONE OF THE MOST novel and insightful safety books you'll ever pick up. Tim Ludwig is a subject matter expert in behavioral safety as well as a great storyteller. Many times he makes his points using real-world (or close to it) stories, and we all know storytelling is one of the best forms of communication and teaching.

What's novel about Tim's book is the points he makes. Safety programs forever have been blighted by dysfunctional practices, very often practiced without the knowledge of how damaging they are. As Tim explains, we're all human and we're doing just what comes naturally. In safety, that includes labeling people as "stupid," "plain lazy," and many other stickers we are so quick to stamp on people, really without giving it much thought. This book explains the damage wrought by blaming the victim as well as any safety work I've read. The unintended impact incurred by the common safety "fishing for faults expeditions" is explained thoughtfully in chapter four and should be thought-provoking for any reader. I couldn't agree more with Tim's point that finding fault with individuals is indeed a serious dysfunctional practice learned by too many managers.

Another important point: Tim clears up the misrepresentation that behavior-based safety focuses on bad behavior and the actions of individuals. The book does an excellent job of explaining how behavior is shaped by systems and environments and organizational cultures. You won't come across a better description of what actually constitutes a "system" in all its components and complexity than you will read in chapter nine.

Tim also executes clear and concise, reader-friendly descriptions of how our brains work (neuroscience), how behavioral science's antecedents and consequences work, how safety cultures work, and how best to observe someone at work and break down their actions into definable, operational definitions that everyone will understand and learn from. Of more importance, you're given solutions to break some of these habitual practices and develop best practices for building sustainable safety cultures, engaging the workforce, and getting the most from behavior-based safety programs and safety management systems.

I think what you'll also find novel about this book is simply its language. This is not a textbook. It's down to earth, funny, sardonic, at times hear-warming; full of stories and characters, deadly serious and also a bit irreverent, and easy to read. It has a tone all its own; one that's unique in the large library of safety literature. Enjoy and embrace it.

Dave Johnson
Editor, *Industrial Safety & Hygiene News*

Preface

A MAN FINDS HIMSELF ON THE TOP STEP of a step ladder; a woman removes the guard to her machine; a worker is not wearing her safety glasses in the plant; a roustabout uses the wrong sized clamp instead of retrieving the right tool from the supply truck; a supervisor teaches a new worker to take short cuts; a mechanic climbs on top of the active machine to find the oil leak. Why do these folks do these things? Is it because they are stupid?

One tendency is to blame workers for safety errors and label their personal failings as the cause of the error. Labeling does not solve problems that cause error and, frankly, it may all be an illusion of human perception leading us to false conclusions. Our human tendencies result in interactions that hurt the safety of our workers and the effectiveness of the systems we put in place to protect them.

These tendencies build dysfunctional management practices that create fear associated with your safety programs. I want to teach you a better way to analyze the behaviors of your employees to understand why they were put in a position to take the risk in the first place. Your system may be perfectly designed to promote risks and create safety traps. By analyzing the context of behavior we can discover ways to change your system to optimize safe behavior and reduce injury. This book presents new ideas and methods using stories we can all relate to.

Human behavior is at the crux of your safety program. Physics and chemistry create hazards ready to be released when things go wrong. Human behavior happens right before that release. Therefore, we look at the behavior associated with the resulting injury and blame the person as the root cause. We label the person "stupid" and feel we have solved the problem. We haven't. Instead, a dysfunctional practice creeps into our safety management system blinding us from finding the true root causes of at-risk behavior.

Labeling, such as calling someone stupid, is a short cut when explaining the behavior of others. As humans, we are really good at fooling ourselves with the short cuts wired in our brains. We can blind ourselves from useful analyses when we use our intuition to explain, rationalize, and make attributions of other's behavior. Our prior experiences, biases, and expectations take us down an illusionary path that may be quite different from reality. This human wiring shapes all of us in ways that further blind us from seeing the true causes of human performance.

A worker's response to derogatory labeling is predictable and automatic, even when the labeling is not specifically directed at them. Labeling creates a workplace-wide culture of fear. Our body physically responds to negative labeling and threats of discipline with a visceral alarm that creates a black cloud over safety programs. It is an anxiety response that workers actively avoid. Who wouldn't? If our goal is to create a safety culture in which workers are engaged with situational awareness, peer coaching, and reporting, we will fail. Our offensive labeling will create avoidance of the very engagement we desperately need from our workers.

We can't fix people, let's not be that pompous. But we can change behavior… we know how; there is a science behind it. We want to define behaviors in a way that are as open to unbiased analysis as the elements of physics and chemistry. Behavior is not a static variable of study. It's not a geologic formation changing over the epoch of time. Behavior is a dynamic variable, reacting with each passing moment along predictable paths, like water in a river, but always ready and able to jump its banks and forge new paths.

We will discover that behavior is neutral, not good or bad, right or wrong. We will learn that for every safe behavior you want from your workers, there are a plethora of competing alternative behaviors that can put them at-risk. What determines this decision is predominantly the work context and your management systems.

With this perspective we can better ask what put the worker in a position to take the risk. We will build an alternative to labeling with dispassionate, actionable and effective analyses to help build the system that helps workers discriminate the best behaviors for the situation.

Easier said than done? Certainly. But can we walk-the-talk? I offer a personal story as a postlude to our book as an example of how hard it can be.

This book is for managers who seek to shape their safety culture to drive out fear and engage their workforce as they drive out risk. I want to help leaders at the top break through their biases and look at safety through a different, more effective lens. Similarly, this book is for the noble safety professional who must build safety management systems to avoid biases and other human tendencies; systems that focus on the controls, PPE, senior leadership involvement, and adequate safety resources that shape and maintain safe behaviors.

Finally, I dedicate this book to the courageous workers who are in the best position to help their sisters and brothers by applying the principles we will discover together. You have been my teachers, your worksites my classroom. You are the everyday heroes deserving of our respect. I wrote this for you.

Tim Ludwig

PART 1:
DYSFUNCTIONAL PRACTICES

WARNING

CHAPTER 1:

You Can't Fix Stupid

IT'S QUITE EASY TO GIVE OURSELVES LABELS, ISN'T IT? Let me explain.

I live up in the mountains and I drive very curvy roads to work and back, to go to the grocery store, kids' basketball games, anywhere. I can go an entire trip without even seeing another car. I've gotten pretty good handling these roads. I have to, they are hazardous.

I live a full two hours from a major city. It's where I head when I go to the airport, big concerts, and to vacation. On this occasion I was doing all three and my family was coming with me. We were in two cars; I drove one and my wife the other because I was flying out after the weekend and she was heading back with the kids. She was following me and I gazed frequently in the rear view mirror to assure myself we were together as the city traffic increased. I'm a mountain driver and the multi-lane highways, constant lights, and excessive traffic had me unnerved. Sure enough, I took a wrong turn and found myself in neighborhood with no sign of my wife in the rearview. I lost her. Fortunately, my phone navigation app got me back to the main road. As I turned on the main road, wondering where my wife was, I glanced at the rear view and, to my astonishment and delight, she was right behind me again!

As I stared into the rear view mirror waving at her I blew right through a big red light. I drove right into five lanes feeding the intersection in four directions. It was sheer luck that no one else was in the intersection. You know that moment when you knew you screwed up? I knew I just I screwed up. Just in case I wasn't aware of my error, an SUV coming from my left laid on his horn and came up right up beside me. I looked over at him. He stared at me with an angry face yelling at the closed windows. All I could do was point at my head with a crooked face and mouth *"I'm stupid."* He seemed to accept that. He nodded, and then he went on. I had interpreted my own behavior with a label, "Stupid," and that simple adjective seemed appropriate. Incidentally, my wife and kids agreed as well.

Labels are Easy

I had stamped myself "stupid." It's quite easy to give ourselves a label, isn't it? We look at our behavior, see the outcome of it, and we give ourselves a label. In fact, labeling is quite popular in modern business where management training often involves some personality test like the *Colors* or the *MBTI* (*Myers Briggs Type Inventory*) where we learn everyone's label in hopes of better collaboration. We are taught to describe ourselves: "I'm an 'Introvert' which explains my discomfort working in big teams;" or "My co-worker is a 'Judger' which explains why she is so critical." Somehow these labels seem to be the magic elixir that makes business work better. We have the impression that if we just "know" ourselves and others better then our work together will be more collaborative and productive. That somehow through a label we can better anticipate how the boss will react to our request for a budget increase for a safety project or we can better manage the resistance we experience from workers given a new safety process.

But, in the end, labeling doesn't impact our ability to manage the behavior of others (or ourselves for that matter). After the labeling event — where we take a survey, learn our color or type (our label) and discuss our tendencies in a group kumbaya, trust-fall session — everyone goes back to the same work environment they came from. We go back to the same deadlines, confusing instructions, boring repetitive tasks, bureaucratic requirements, inferior tools, degrading facilities, and dealing with the same ambiguity that make human interactions complicated. The environment is the context of all we do. It is not one thing, it is a multitude of present realities and artifacts of past events of varying levels of importance that our brain has to navigate and engage with. This dynamic and complex environment triggers our actions and afterward lets us know if our actions made a difference, or just screwed up things more. After labeling, we may feel enlightened, but the environment doesn't change and we end up acting the same way as in the past as the environment dictated. Nothing changes.

But we don't need an intense labeling session to be labelers. We do it all the time as a human tendency. Consider this question: Don't we overuse labels when dealing with the safety of our work crews and managers? For example, if workers can't follow rules and procedures that are clearly written in the manuals and training, and then they get hurt, they're "Stupid," "Noncompliant," or "Lazy" or "_____" (you can fill in the blank — please keep it rated "PG-13"). Shoot, we even label when folks don't get hurt, such as when their work space is disorganized or PPE disheveled, when they have blank eyes during a safety meeting or hide their errors. We label a lot... and it's a dysfunctional practice. Let me explain...

The Stupid Manager

I was invited to go to an automobile parts plant that had a lot of safety issues. Their injury rate was too high and a new general manager was brought in — young guy. He had been there for about a half a year and, from all accounts, he had been doing a really good job of just picking the low-hanging fruit. You know, putting guards on hazardous equipment, upgrading PPE, writing some SOPs, and cleaning up stuff.

I was there to do a safety culture assessment. I had assembled a focus group of line employees and some maintenance folks in a front office board room, seeking to understand why their team's safety culture scored the most negative in the whole corporation on a recent survey. The general manager and safety pro were also in the board room with us. One of the problems they talked about was they had a lot of aging machinery that would mist and drip a lot of oil. The conversation started quite diplomatic when everyone acknowledged that things had gotten better. It used to be they couldn't even see the clock on the wall because of the oil mist in the air.

The manager had put in filtration systems and some "band aids" on the machines. He had been working hard at it and the employees did say they appreciated his work, although I could tell they definitely still had some unspoken grievances about working conditions. But the manager didn't reciprocate this diplomacy. In fact, when I got him talking more honestly (I am a psychologist after all) the manager showed his frustration. His hands were animated when he said, *"I've done all I can. The workers just don't care. I'm spending tens of thousands of dollars fixing equipment and our facilities, but the workers just don't care. They just don't get it. They keep doing idiotic things and get hurt. There's something wrong with them. It's something in the head."*

One of the workers, a redhead woman, was sitting at the other end of the table. I remember her vividly; she was stewing and shifting in her seat until she bravely blurted out, *"YOU CALLING US STUPID?"* Not a moment passed as he looked at her and said, *"Stupid is as stupid does."* I was aghast. My mouth was open. Did he just say that? So I knew something was about to go down. Predictably, the room blew up and their negative safety culture was emerging right in front of me as they argued about blame and labels in the oh-so-typical "we vs. they" entrenchments.

The implication was, if workers can't follow the rules... policies, manuals, procedures, training... they're stupid. The manager threw down the label, STUPID, in the board room in front of everybody.

But you know what? *You can't fix stupid.* That's why the manager was so frustrated; he couldn't fix this human problem as easily as he could the machines. He was frustrated because he used a label to describe behavior: "You employees are stupid."

What can you do about Stupid? Honestly, what can you do? Do you coach the person taking risks? That rarely works because they may try to comply with your logic and requests but find themselves back in the same environment once you leave. Do you fire the "stupid" person? Then you're going to hire someone just as... stupid. They will end up frustrating you as well because they will be put in the same environment as the exiting person. So you're left with no solution when you label, except getting more and more upset, pleading with workers, "Don't be stupid."

Telling folks "Don't BE this..." simply does not work. You can't fix a label; that would be like fixing a person. Instead of asking a person to BE or NOT TO BE something, focus on how you can help them DO what is required to be safe.

I had had enough of the arguing. It was time for me to have confidential discussions with the group of workers, which is part of my process. This gave me an opportunity to kick the manager out. The manager left the room for about an hour-and-a-half. When he came back around lunchtime, he was ashen. He had no color in his face. He was visibly shaken, definitely embarrassed. He had his head down. The redheaded woman noticed and asked, *"What's going on, sir?"* To his credit, he was honest. He said, *"You know, I decided, I blocked the whole day for this focus group. I didn't anticipate this extra time, so I decided to go back to my office and get caught up in email. I wanted to keep my eye on the ball and figure out what you folks are talking about when you complain about the plant and your work. You were challenging me to put myself in your shoes so I took that opportunity to go out and work in the plant... to see what you guys are talking about.*

"I'm no laborer and I'm not a machinist, so I don't want to go out and mess things up by working on or around the machines. So I thought I'd do maintenance." He joked, *"Even a manager can change light bulbs."* That's what he did. There was one area of the plant that was dark, so he got some bulbs and went to work. The manager paused and took a deep breath, avoiding eye contact, and continued, *"Well, before I knew it, I found myself with one foot on the top of the step ladder, on the tip of my toe reaching for the light bulb on the ceiling. My other knee was up on piping trying to get more lift."* The step ladder

kicked off, he slid on the oily pipe, but somehow grabbed the pipe and stopped the fall. He was then able to climb down. It had just happened before he returned to the board room.

The redhead jumped up, right out of her seat, *"What are you... stupid?"* It was funny, everyone laughed. They were showing him: *"You label us and we label you. What are you going to do now?"* He simply agreed, *"Yeah, I was stupid."*

A Better Analysis

I took the opportunity to insert some behavioral science, do a smarter analysis, and teach them how to change behavior. Trying to gain control, I pulled the flip chart over and did an analysis of the situation. We first described the behavior that put him at-risk: standing on top of a step ladder. We then asked the manager, *"Why did you do it?"* He predictably replied, *"Well, it was stupid."*

Incident- Fell off Stepladder

Antecedents ("In this situation")
• 6- foot ladder at the loading dock
• Step ladder was right there

Safe Behavior ("If I act this way")
    Get a 6-foot ladder

Consequences ("Then this will happen to me")
• Avoid falling
• 15 minute walk to and from the loading dock   Falling is not likely
• Exposure to machinery and oil while carrying the 6-foot ladder
                            Extra effort and exposure is very likely

I asked *"Can we fix stupid?"* The group looked perplexed, they couldn't fix stupid... after all this was their manager. I finally said, *"Instead of trying to fix your manager here let's actually focus on something we can fix. So let's consider, why did he find himself on the top rung of a step ladder? How did he end up in the position to take this risk? Let's figure this out and we'll have something to fix."*

"The at-risk behavior was 'standing on top of a step ladder', why did he do this?" The manager took the first stab at the question saying that the step ladder he used was in a housekeeping closet about 20 steps away.

"OK, then what was the safer alternative?" The maintenance manager offered his expertise, *"For that height, you should use a six-foot ladder."* So that begged the question, *"Why did he choose the step ladder over the six-foot ladder?"*

We noted that the proper ladder, the six-foot ladder, was located at the shipping dock. To get to the shipping dock the manager would have had to walk all the way through the factory, about a seven-minute walk (times two for the round trip). Imagine that. He'd have to walk across the factory and then back through all that hazardous oily machinery carrying a six-foot ladder… just to change that light bulb. Getting the six-foot ladder was costly in terms of effort. You would have to walk for about 15 minutes through the plant and be exposed to more hazards.

We call this a "response cost" and it factors into our decision to do the safe action or take a short cut that may put us at-risk. When we engage in a behavior there are consequences. Some behaviors take extra time that could have been used elsewhere; extra effort that makes us more fatigued; or behaviors may even have social consequences, such as tarnishing our reputation or trust among fellow workers. These all "cost" us and, naturally, we try to minimize costs.

So, simple question: Do you think the extra response cost associated with getting the six-foot ladder encouraged or discouraged using the right tool for the job? You'd only have to walk through the plant a couple times with heavy objects to experience the response cost and begin avoiding similar trips in the future. In technical terms, the behaviors involved in getting the correct ladder are punished due to this response cost. Behavior avoids punishment. So the manager didn't go get that ladder.

What alternative do you have if he did not retrieve the six-foot ladder? Well, he could not fix the light bulb. Not an option. Another alternative was that he could simply walk right over to the available step ladder in the cleaning closet and use it. This would only take a couple seconds, it's not that heavy, and he could get the job done quicker.

You'd only have to execute the easier, more convenient option a couple times to begin to choose doing so in the future. The behaviors involved in getting the incorrect ladder are reinforced due to this low response cost. Behavior seeks out reinforcement. So the manager used the step ladder.

We discovered very quickly that the circumstances surrounding the ladder encouraged the risk. Getting the job done quicker and easier was the more powerful consequence. We arrived at the root cause.

It was one of those "easy button" moments. Managers love the easy button. Our manager hit the table, *"We'll procure ladders and put them in the housekeeping closets around the plant. Heck, yeah."*

We also discovered we did not have to call each other stupid. We did not have to label. Indeed, we can't fix stupid, but we can fix the situation! Our analysis allowed us to arrive at a solution: make the safe behavior quicker and easier to do. We didn't fix stupid, we didn't have to because no one was actually stupid. We proposed to fix the environment and were certain now that this would change behavior. Future workers would be more likely to use the correct ladder.

This solution was made even easier because they had originally created these housekeeping closets because of the oil problem. They needed people to mop the floors when there were oil spills. Housekeeping closets, equipped with a mop and water and a pail, were built all over the plant. All that needed to be done to promote safe ladder use was to procure the six-foot ladders and put them in the closets. This pleased the maintenance guys around the table who had been asking for these for years. Easy button.

We had reached a solution! This cheered up the focus group and they started talking about other things to put in these housekeeping closets so their tools would be in closer proximity to where they need them. But when we started talking about the oily floors, the manager started to sulk. He stood up and interrupted, *"Those mop and the pails in the housekeeping closets, workers don't use them. I've been trying to clean up the oil problem since I got here and all I'm asking you workers to do is to clean up the floor when you see spills. But you're NOT doing this. I still see oil on the floor all over the plant. YOU PEOPLE ARE LAZY."*

Another label: You're lazy.

The redhead woman, much calmer now, stopped him, *"Sir. Yes we have mops and pails... and yes, we mop. We tried it, sir, but it didn't work. See, after we finish mopping the water the pail is all oily. The next person that uses the mop gets the oily water. After a while, we're just taking the oil mopped up from before and putting it back on the floor."*

The manager was dumbfounded. *"Change the water. If you changed the water, you wouldn't be putting oil back on the floor."* You could almost hear the manager say "Duh!" under his breath.

The redhead said calmly, *"Sir, where's the plumbing? Where's the hose for the clean water?"* Guess where it was. It was all the way back at the loading dock where they clean the trucks. To get clean water, a worker would have to push a pail full of oily water through the machinery to the loading dock to change out the water, and then come all the way back with the clean water. More than 15 minutes would be wasted (they were still on the clock); they would be more exposed to hazards while exposing others as well. So they didn't do it.

Again, we didn't need to label. I could have let them argue about who was stupid or who was lazy for the whole day. But that is counterproductive. Instead, we stopped labeling and started a smarter analysis of the environment that put people in the position to take risks. The lesson learned here: instead of labeling, make the proper tools more available at the point where the work is done. Change the environment, and by changing the environment, we change behavior. Workers should no longer have to find themselves in a situation that encourages them to take risks. By the end of our focus group, the manager was talking about how to retrofit plumbing throughout the factory.

Instead of asking a person to BE something, focus on how you can help them DO what is required to be safe. Recognize that EVERYONE wants to be safe and act safe. It is your job to remove the barriers that put them in the position to, knowingly or unknowingly, take that risk. When you get away from the label, you'll be much more likely to see what those barriers are.

Labeling is a human tendency that, as we saw, results in a dysfunctional practice that not only hurts your safety culture but also does little to reduce the risks that get people hurt. Indeed, folks at the auto parts plant were at each other's throats forcefully agreeing that safety was a problem but actively blaming each other instead of working together on a solution. In our next chapter, let's take a hard look at blaming. Let's discover why it occurs, and how it grows into another dysfunctional practice that has a way of getting inserting into our safety management systems, substantially degrading effectiveness.

> Instead of asking a person to BE something, focus on how you can help them DO what is required to be safe.

DYSFUNCTIONAL PRACTICE: LABELING

Labeling is a natural human tendency. "Stupid" is a label, no one is stupid. Labeling starts arguments and entrenches people against each other.

You can't fix a label. After labeling, we may feel enlightened, but the environment doesn't change and we end up acting the same way as in the past as the environment dictated. Nothing changes. Labeling hurts our ability to manage the behaviors of others.

We should attempt to change the environment, not the person. Instead of asking a person to BE something, focus on how you can help them DO what is required to be safe.

CHAPTER 2:
Blaming the Worker

A Lesson Not Learned

WE LEARNED A LESSON IN THAT OILY PLANT. Unfortunately, the next story is a lesson not learned. It was a close call that eventually ended up resulting in injury.

I was asked by a large multinational oil and gas company to teach them some behavioral science during their annual meeting in Dubai. Fighting off jetlag, I told them the story of the oily plant and risk-taking manager, concluding, in part, that we should not blame the worker when risks are discovered or injuries suffered. I told them if they wanted to take advantage of behavioral science to reduce injuries, don't use labels. Instead, they need to understand the context of the behavior and why that worker was put in the position to take the risk. It was not the easiest concept to grasp but these were Environment, Health, & Safety (EHS) executives from all over the world and some of the smartest people I've worked with. We had a productive workshop.

I could tell they were still mulling over the concept when we went out to a special dinner. Now, as you know, I'm from a rural southern mountain town with rolling country roads, so being in the midst of Arab opulence in Dubai was quite heady. Our host had arranged for us to eat under a veranda looking over a pond that extended to the tallest fountain in the world exploding to the tunes of Whitney Houston. Behind this spectacle you have the tallest building in the world. It was a perfect Arabian night. We enjoyed nice wine, a steak, and I was absorbed in it all.

Executives must plan these moments because just when I was fully absorbed in this Arabian magic my host, in charge of EHS for all the Middle East for this multinational company, grabbed my attention *"Tim, let me ask you a question. In your workshop today you taught that we shouldn't blame the worker. We appreciate what you taught us. But let me tell you a story."*

This company was heavily engaged in fracking. A lot of piping holds enormous amounts of pressure in a fracking operation. This is not fixed piping. As a worker you're going out to a field location and assembling dozens of hoses and pumps from the back of flat beds. Then you go about the process of fracking, repairing, fracking, and repairing. All the while a "company man" is watching and charging tens of thousands of dollars against your contract if you have "non-productive time" due to an error or delay. At the end of this week-long odyssey the well is now producing and you're disassembling the whole complex, still under the eye of the company man who now wants you gone so they can begin the next stage of construction.

Part of process when you're breaking down is removing the hoses from the huge pumps on the back of flatbed trucks. When you're fracking, you produce lot of pressure that is sent underground, so when you're breaking the hose and pump assemblies down you have to make sure there's no pressure in these hoses. If there is, horrible things can happen.

Even though the engineers remove the pressure from all of the hoses, it is important that the field operator do a double check on each hose before they decouple it. There's a two-minute process, where field operators check the local pressure of the hose pressure and, if necessary, bleed it out fully before opening the coupling and removing the hose. This exercise is done based on the one in ten-thousand chance that there may still be latent pressure hiding in the hose.

After this process was explained, I was told a tale about a supervisor who was decoupling hoses on his own. He had been with the company a long time so he had done this task many times. He was fatigued, being in the field doing 12-hour shifts, and ready to get back to base. The company man wanted them out of the way, so he was in a hurry to finish the job. He had his full team decoupling hoses and was behind the trucks doing it himself.

As he decoupled hoses he took a short cut by skipping over the two-minute pressure test. He had done this hundreds of times in the past and never blew a coupling because there was inevitably no pressure in the hose.

Unfortunately, this time he opened the coupling and there was latent pressure waiting for him. The casing exploded and sent a projectile through the cab of the flatbed truck holding the pump. Fortunately, no one was in the cab.

Shocked at this story, I asked, *"Was he okay? Was everybody okay?"* Everybody was okay. I was curious about the incident so I started asking questions. Yes, the pressure check was in the Standard Operating Procedures; yes, it was on the break-down checklist and reviewed in the Job Safety Analysis (J.S.A.). I kept asking questions but my host stopped me, *"No, Tim, no. I haven't finished my story."*

Three years later, this same supervisor was teaching a Green Hat how to decouple hoses out in the field. "Green Hat" is the name they called new workers because they made them wear green hard hats to distinguish them from experienced employees — a way of keeping an eye on these novice workers. The Green Hats had learned at the training facility how to decouple hoses under controlled conditions. But they were now out in the field, the real world with real reality such as weather, stuck couplings, and production pressures. They had to decouple hoses first with supervision present before they were certified to do it on their own.

In the EHS manager's story, I learned that the supervisor who nearly got hurt three years earlier was teaching his Green Hats "how we really do it." He was working with one Green Hat and instructed him to skip the pressure check, saying it was unnecessary and time-consuming. All was going well until later in the day when physics and chemistry were not so forgiving. The one-of-ten-thousand happened and there was still energy in the hose. When the Green Hat decoupled this hose the casing exploded. Unfortunately, this time the projectile ricocheted off the pump and struck the young man in the head. After an emergency evacuation they found he suffered permanent brain damage. Horrible incident.

"Tim," finger pointing at me by my EHS host, *"how can you tell me we do not blame that supervisor?"* Indeed, the supervisor had taken a short cut three years earlier and barely escaped a serious injury. He should have learned. Three years later he taught somebody else to take the same short cut and that young man's life will never be the same.

"*How can we not blame him, Tim?*" Suddenly, Dubai and all its opulence fell away. I had to explain myself and defend my science in the face of this tragedy.

The others around the table started chiming in. The word "stupid" wasn't the only label being applied. There were other labels offered like "incompetent," "reckless," and "rebellious." Some were not pretty and uttered in languages native to the EHS manager but I got the picture. I'd be upset too. We were talking about a person whose intentional actions hurt someone else under his watch.

Now I had ten people around me waiting for an answer. They were dedicated EHS professionals, the likes of which I respect beyond measure, doing things for their workforce that were so impressive I was frankly in awe of them. And here they were, at wit's end about human behavior.

There are times as an expert when you don't know the answer. In those situations you start asking questions. You ask questions to understand the context in hopes of getting to the root of the problem — but the answer is often hidden. This is why safety pros suggest asking the "Five Whys" because you need to ask at least five questions to get to the root cause. So I asked questions to learn more, but, to be honest, I needed time to think.

My questions took them back to the original event, when the supervisor was by himself, blew the casing off and damaged some equipment. I asked, *"What happened after that?"*

"He got coached." I was not surprised by this answer. Coaching is common practice in safety. The answer to rule violations is often coaching and training and retraining. Regardless, in this case I imagine the coaching was pretty forceful and threatening.

"Yeah, okay, he got coached." I reflected, "Did that change his behavior?"

The answer was obviously "no." This supervisor was still taking and teaching a risk three years later. This is the problem with coaching. It is often a formal process where the infraction is met with a formal, documented description of the infraction and a verbal reprimand. This document would then be described as the "first strike" toward discipline, such as unpaid days off or termination. However, nothing changes in the environment that caused the risk to be taken in the first place. Also, the supervisor would have to get caught violating the rules again, something that is highly unlikely. So his behavior may have complied with the rules for the next couple weeks after the coaching. But his behavior would drift back to what his immediate environment dictated, so much so that he was actually teaching the short cut.

So I continued with my questioning: *"What else happened after the first incident?"* The response came as a matter of fact: *"We filled out the incident reports. We wrote him up and made it a Hi-Po. A Hi-Po is a close call that gets sent all the way to our top executives because of the potential severity of the incident. His first incident went all the way to the top; it got everybody's attention."*

"OK," I asked, *"then what?"*

"What do you mean?"

"You said you did this Hi-Po, right? So I assume you filled out a form detailing the results of an investigation. I'm sure that somewhere on the form, hopefully, there's a big square with the conclusion as to the root cause of the Hi-Po incident. This big square should highlight what we've got to fix so it doesn't happen again."

"So, what was the root cause?" My host, palms out, replied matter-of-factly, *"Human error."* Translation: *"He was stupid."*

The Incident happened the first time and no one was hurt. The supervisor got coached but that didn't change his behavior. Probably a dozen people did an investigation to complete this important form, taking hours, if not days, of everybody's time. The final conclusion: "Stupid."

Then what happened? Nothing happened. You Can't Fix Stupid.

The Bad Habit of Root Causes

I've had the opportunity to go around the world to assess the behavioral impact of different companies' safety management systems, such as their incident investigations, close call and minor injury reporting, and behavior-based safety (BBS) observations. I always ask to see their forms used to investigate incidents — be they injuries, Hi-Po's or even peer-to-peer observations in BBS.

I recall an exciting trip down under to visit Australian gold mines. I was very impressed with their online incident investigation system. An incident anywhere in the world is recorded, analyzed, and shared throughout their mines so others may learn from these lessons. It was a state-of-the-art system where even a miner could log in and register the most minor incidents. Clearly this company intended to understand the root cause of the incident and get the word out. Even though the company worked on nearly every continent, the hazards and risks of mining are pretty much the same anywhere you go (and we went about everywhere). Thus, if a team learns something in one location it will benefit hundreds of other teams around the globe.

I had a chance to enter a fictional incident into their online incident investigation system. The right questions were asked around weather, production cycle, tools and equipment, and supervision. Instead of being a long, cumbersome form that discouraged reporting, the online form was elegant and short — the safety pros would follow up with more intensive descriptions. The last screen of the online form was title "Root Cause" and featured a pull-down list to choose a single definitive cause for the incident. The very first item? "Human Error." Translation: "Stupid."

I asked for a report from the unit manager listing the reporting from the previous quarter. They had an impressive culture of reporting. Minor injuries and near misses were abundant. However, when I found the page on root causes I found that "Human Error" was listed on more than 70 percent of the reports. It had sucked the wind out of the process. On the next page were lessons learned and tactics to share with other mines. Because "Human Error" was listed so copiously the only tactics that came out of the report tended to be training and "awareness session" stand-downs.

The way we try to fix a problem that is based upon a label is to try and fix the person, and we are bad at it. We rely on "telling" people what to do and why to do it. We do this in many forms. We do it through training and coaching; we do it in meetings and personal conversations; we do it through signs and instruction manuals; through rule books and standard operating procedures.

All of these are forms of exhortation. The famous management guru (and one of my heroes — look him up!) W. Edwards Deming decried the use of exhortations. The definition of exhortation, according to Google, is *"a communication emphatically urging someone to do something,"* its Latin origin is the word for "pleading." We overuse exhortations in our training, in our incident investigation summaries shared with workers, and in our personal conversations. In safety a lot of what workers are told is "Do this;" "This is the safe way to do this;" follow these rules, instructions, etc. Exhortations may direct behavior, telling people what to do, but they don't motivate behavior because they don't change the consequences of behavior in the environment. All the ways we try to fix people have the right intentions but are ultimately insufficient.

I've seen the exhortation phenomena in particular over and over and over in nearly every industry. Even the best safety programs in the world suffer from this dysfunctional practice. I was assessing a behavioral safety program at a petroleum refinery to determine if they were to become accredited by a not-for-profit named the Cambridge Center for Behavioral Studies (Behavior.org) of which I'm a trustee. The refinery was impressive, generating more than 30,000 voluntary observations a year from their 700+ employees and contractors. They had a go-to database to analyze these observations and share trends with their numerous employee BBS teams who ran the program.

> Exhortations may direct behavior, telling people what to do, but they don't motivate behavior because they don't change the consequences of behavior in the environment.

Even their observation cards were innovative. These cards went past the typical behavioral check sheet of potential safe and at-risk behaviors. On the back was a list of possible causes of the at-risk behavior observed. I thought it was cool that they called these causes "barriers." Barriers were blocking safe behaviors. Removing these barriers would allow a worker to pursue the safe alternative. This mindset is very much in line with behavioral science.

Yet, I began to look over their card and the very first item on the barriers checklist was "Personal Choice." Translation: "I was stupid." We looked into how many times "Personal Choice" was checked after an at-risk behavior was identified and found that more than 65 percent of their 30,000 observation cards had it checked as the cause of the behavior. Of course they made a bad choice, they put themselves at risk.

They were not being stupid; they were making the best choices within the environment and prior experience they possessed at the time. Only afterward, when the risk is pointed out do they look at what may have happened and conclude, "Stupid." But that doesn't get us anywhere.

This observation data was rolled up and trended and the findings went out to the BBS teams to use as they built interventions to increase safe behaviors. More than 65 percent of the risks were supposedly due to "Personal Choice." What do you do with "Personal Choice"? Not much. The product of all their observations, all their data analysis, all this team's work ended up only producing one "awareness session" after another, exhorting workers not to do the at-risk behavior. Exhortation (Latin translation: *pleading*) doesn't work, as I've stated. These awareness sessions seemed to work. The at-risk behavior dropped when they analyzed follow-up observations — but only for the next weeks or two. Then the behavior would drift back into the same pattern as before. Unfortunately, by then, the BBS team had thought the problem was solved and moved on, leaving the risk, and the environment that caused the risk, in place unchanged.

Also, after enough pleading sessions some dysfunctional things happen. First, the informative awareness session goes from explaining to demanding. After a period of time the safety pro (or BBS facilitators) get frustrated that their exhortations don't work. But instead of taking on a different tactic they double down on the exhortation with stronger language and perhaps even threats. Guess what this dysfunctional practice does to a safety culture? Workers get "hardened," demands don't get heeded, threats don't get acted upon, and the exhortations fall on deaf ears.

Let's summarize: Labeling is not a root cause and the solutions generated from labels, such as coaching or awareness sessions, are likely to be ineffective. We try to change the person and that rarely works. Nothing really changes, the behavior remains and injuries continue as evidenced by our story of the supervisor whose behavior caused a serious brain injury to a Green Hat. Let's rejoin that story…

The Hi-Po was a No-Show

The oil services' EHS Hi-Po report concluded "Human Error" as the cause of the supervisor's first incident where he blew off the casing of a high-pressure hose after taking a shortcut in the fracking fields. Then nothing happened. The Hi-Po was filed, the supervisor was coached, and the work went on, only to have the risk repeated by this supervisor. How many times did he take this same risk over the next three years? How many people did he teach to take the same short cut over the next three years?

Let's step back further. Who had taught him to take the risk? How many others had been taught to take the risk as well?

The work went on after the first Hi-Po Incident only to have the risk repeated — by how many people? His company is more than 100,000 workers strong. Fracking services are one of their biggest units. Tens of thousands of workers just like him do the same task all the time. How many people worldwide are taking the shortcut exactly the way he was doing?

The root cause was not him. It remained elsewhere, undiscovered and untouched, hidden behind the illusion that they had reached a root cause when all they had done was exonerate their responsibility to find a real solution by slapping a label on the problem.

At that Dubai restaurant, we concluded that the real root cause of the second incident, the one where the young man was struck in the head by the ricocheting casement, that root cause was a faulty Hi-Po incident investigation process had that failed to find a real solution when incidents like this had occurred in the past.

Indeed, the real reasons that caused the incident were still in place. The contracts, the equipment, the processes or procedures didn't change. To the worker, it just didn't make sense to take those extra minutes to check the residual pressure on every single hose they were decoupling while engaged in the dozens of other tasks involved in breaking down a fracking site. All the while moving with the speed that will make the company man happy and get them back to the comfortable air-conditioned base faster.

The Hi-Po did not consider the circumstances associated with taking the short cut. Certainly the consequences of taking a short cut were extreme. Your behavior could cause an explosion that could severely injure yourself or someone else. At best, you'd come in contact with discipline and coaching. But these consequences were not probable. You could go your whole career taking this short cut and not experience an incident.

The consequence of taking the shortcut could also be discipline. The supervisor and anyone who put their lives or the lives of others in harm's way need to come in contact with discipline and possible removal for their actions. And certainly this supervisor will suffer the rest of his days with the memory of his actions causing serious harm to another. Indeed, discipline is required in these situations and can be an effective deterrent in safety management systems when used fairly and consistently.

So coaching and discipline should keep you from taking the risk. But is discipline a probable outcome, enough to be a deterrent? Most of the time the answer is "no." In order for discipline to work, the disciplinarian needs to: a) be present at the time of the rule violation and not stuck in an office doing email or at a meeting full of exhortations; b) see the rule violation and not have eyes fixed on some clipboard checklist completing a form; and c) choose to go through the awkward and lengthy process of confronting the worker, completing more forms, dealing with human resources, and experiencing the inevitable backlash from the work team. At best, the supervisor will take a moment to threaten the worker with an exhortation and a mean look. And even then, workers will perceive that discipline is only dolled out to those out-of-favor employees who have found themselves on the wrong side of the supervisor. The favored ones always get a pass. So workers learn that discipline is not consistent. Bottom line: it is often an ineffective method of changing behavior.

Keep in mind that, in our story, it was the supervisor himself who was both taking the shortcut and teaching it to others. The deviance had been normalized. Certainly, workers who see this know that discipline is off the table for this rule and that the real way of doing things bends the rule.

Now lets get real.

The engineers who designed the two-minute pressure check and wrote the SOPs certainly thought what they were asking was minuscule and reasonable. Two minutes is the time it takes to get a drink of water. But these field operators were not just decoupling one hose. They had more than 100 hoses to decouple when breaking down a fracking site. The two-minute pressure check being requested would culminate in 200+ extra minutes to finish that step in the break-down process. That's more than three extra hours. Keep in mind that this was not the only safety step that took extra time during the break-down process — there were dozens ranging from pre-task briefings and parts inspections to hoisting preparations and load securing processes.

If we had gone beyond labeling and rules we would have learned that these frackers were telling us with their short cuts that TIME was a root cause of their at-risk behavior.

The Hi-Po investigation should have gone a different direction. Was there a perception among the field operators and supervisors (and the operations manager and the company man) that the three hours would be non-productive time which may contribute to late schedule fines? This would have led managers to ask a critical question: had those additional three hours been calculated into the work plan that was written into the contract for the work to begin with, or had it been negotiated away? Indeed, the contracting system may have been motivating shortcuts. Yes, the events that took place months earlier between engineers, contracting managers and customer procurement lawyers may have exposed the workers to risks when they codified in the contract the exact time the break down would take and the fines related to tardy performance.

The Hi-Po from the supervisor's actions, and probably many, many more close call reports could have been trended and analyzed to provide the evidence needed for decision-makers to adapt their contracting process to allow for the extra time needed to perform safety checks and other safety processes. These analyses could also lead engineers to design more efficient pressure checks that don't take as long or as much effort. Certainly when engaged in more sober, effective analyses, these oil professionals could get this short cut under control by designing systems to take the error out of the process.

And if they got this one right, imagine how many other risks they can mitigate by trending and analyzing close call reporting to make both proximal changes to the immediate environment (e.g., getting the six-foot ladders closer to where they will be needed) as well as distal changes to higher-order systems such as engineering, planning, and contracting. These would have affected every single of the tens of thousands of workers who do the job. Now we would be talking real actions that produce real decreases in injuries.

Instead, our host company assigned a label as the root cause of the Hi-Po. Instead of giving decision-makers the analyses they needed to make real change, they showed the label to the executives of the company. Everybody now knew that supervisor was stupid. And the work went on…

If you have "Human Error," "Human Factor," or "Stupid" as an option in your incident investigations it is all too easy to just stop there, file the report, do some exhortations, and keep on using the system that caused the risk in the first place.

The safety management system made it too easy to label the supervisor in the Hi-Po and stop there. No meaningful changes were made to the work or, in this case, the upstream systems to the work such as con-tracting that could have stopped the risk from happening. Meaningful change could have spared this one supervisor from teaching a shortcut that later damaged a subordinate for life and eliminated a risk to the entire workforce.

The Hi-Po was a no-show and the incident was forgotten… until three years later.

DYSFUNCTIONAL PRACTICE: BLAMING

Workers are too often blamed for incidents in our incident investigations as well as other processes such as behavior-based safety. The root cause of "Human Error" blames the worker.

When workers are seen as a root cause we over-rely on exhortations like training, coaching, and instructions. Exhortations direct behavior but they don't motivate.

When we blame and try to change the worker through exhortations we leave the real reasons for the incident untouched and hidden.

If the real reasons that caused the incident remain untouched the risk will be repeated over and again by anyone engaging in that task.

CHAPTER 3:

Labels are an Illusion

LABELS GIVE YOU THE ILLUSION, AND IT IS AN ILLUSION folks, that you've reached a root cause when all you've done is exonerate your responsibility to find a real solution.

The emotions of an incident are one reason we use labels. When someone gets hurt or worse, we are slightly relieved when we level blame and assign a label. It's like a catharsis. You safety pros out there know what it feels like to get "that phone call" disrupting your day, evening, or night's sleep. You learn that someone got hurt on your watch. It's like a punch to the gut. You think about the injured, the family, and the crew. Later you begin to think about how the event impacts your program. Your first reaction is guilt; guilt that the injury happened on your watch; guilt that you should have done something about the pain and suffering. This is because you're passionate about keeping people safe and you have a deep sense of caring. It can be traumatic when you first get the call and visit with the victim or survey the site of the injury. Emotions run high.

Your plans for the next week go out the window. Your numbers are affected. This all leads not only to guilt but frustration, especially when the injury seems to be due to personal choices or violations of a safety rule. So we slap a label on the experience. Labeling is like putting the incident in box. Neatly identified and wrapped up it relieves the pressure that comes from those emotions and frustration… a bit.

Labeling eases frustration. It's kind of a defense mechanism for the brain to relieve the functioning of the amygdala. Think about when you're driving and someone cuts you off, forcing you to jam your brake. Your face tightens and teeth clinch while your temper rises. What's the first thing that comes to you mind? A label: "Idiot."

In my personal assessment, when someone cuts me off they are either tagged "idiots" or, um, let's just stay PG and call them "rude-holes." Here's the truth of the matter: Does me uttering "idiot" or (PG) "rude" aloud in my car impact the person in the other car? Certainly not. Then why do we do it? Catharsis.

My favorite label applies to employees who never buy in to anything you try to do in your safety programming. They are labeled CAVEmen (& women), standing for "Citizens Against Virtually Everything." The label tries to account for a complex set of resistance behaviors that always get in the way of good safety programming. CAVEmen piss you off because they are always questioning and poisoning the well behind your back.

What lies behind this behavior is complex and not easily resolved. So, simply and quickly we write them off with a demeaning label. It's a bit amusing and allows for some catharsis.

> Labels give you the illusion that you've reached a root cause when all you've done is exonerate your responsibility to find a real solution.

But labeling is not a solution, not a fix, and we get frustrated again and again with behavior we don't understand.

It may de-stress us, but labeling is an illusion. An illusion is something that looks or seems different than it really is. The illusion here is that our perception of reality around an incident is different than factual reality; the true cause of the incident. Labels are nothing more than mental shortcuts. We try to characterize people, try to define them so we know how to act around them. We toss around labels to try to predict other's actions so we can plan for them. If we label our boss a "stickler" we anticipate her frequent and detailed questioning and therefore over-prepare for those encounters. If we tag someone as "stupid" when it comes to safety, we predict that they will be "accident-prone." When we come to this conclusion we may overdo the handholding and create a lot of rules, put up tons of posters, and stress every detail.

This is how our brains are wired. It is also another way our brain deludes us about reality. The brain has amazing capacity but can only manage limited input. To compensate, our brain conjures up a lot of perceptions of reality for us. When at work or home or wherever, we are swimming in physical stimuli — 300 exebytes (300 billion-billion) to be more specific. Of that, only a fraction get picked up by our senses. It is estimated that 11 million bits of data a second are produced by our sense organs and sent to our brains. Most of this gets processed unconsciously. Now get this: it has been estimated that only 50 bits of information a second make it to our conscious brain, where we have a chance to analyze this information, perceive what's going on, and react. But human experience is much more detailed, complex, and continuous than 50 bits/second.

Much of our perception beyond what our sense organs (11 million bits) can handle is fabricated for us based on past experience and the like. Much of our perceptual reality, our vision, hearing, taste, touch, and smell is our brain's interpretation of physical reality based on the limited information our sense organs can transmute into our neural network. The brain takes short cuts by getting the "gist" of things and producing a reality into our 50 bits of conscious mind.

In essence, neuropsychologists realize that perception is mostly an illusion gifted to us by our brain.

More complex information about the world, such as all of the responsibilities you have to deal with on the job, works in much the same way. Our environment is a complicated place and our brain can only handle so much. Our working memory, what we are conscious of right now, has a processing capacity of 120 bits per second. This amounts to holding only seven plus or minus two pieces of information in consciousness at any one time. We simply don't have the capacity to gather all the constant input about everyone around us. We can't hold that much information in consciousness to analyze thoroughly before we can make a decision. We need to be efficient, we need to act fast, and labels are convenient ways to take a lot of information and distill it down to something simple.

For example, we see the new maintenance guy hired just last week. There is a lot to learn about him. We could look into his application material for his past experiences; we could follow up on references to learn about his safety performance at former jobs; we could observe him doing his new job for a couple hours to get a good feel for his techniques and skills; and we could have extensive conversations with him to better understand his knowledge of hazards and personal concerns and limitations. To get to know a person thoroughly takes a long time. Shoot, sometimes we feel we really don't know our long-time friends or ourselves for that matter, and we've been with ourselves our whole life.

So do we spend a lot of time and effort to get to know all the relevant facets about this new guy in maintenance? Do you even have much time, considering he's only one of your many employees? The answer is most likely "no." Remember, our information processing must be quick and efficient.

This rush to judge via labeling is problematic for two reasons. First, we tend to form our impressions of people, our labels, within the first two minutes of meeting them. Some research suggests we form a label in the first 15 seconds. In my university courses my students rate me during their end-of-the semester course evaluations. This is after about 15 weeks of instruction, about 45 hours of experience with me, their humble professor. Research shows that if you simply gave my students the course evaluation after the first class period (75 minutes), I would get pretty much the same results as I get after a full semester. Researchers at Harvard actually found almost the same results after having students watch only a 15-second video of a professor — without sound! First impressions are everything. The primacy effect is real and it will subsequently bias the rest of your judgment.

We label out of convenience and we do it very quickly on limited information. Keep in mind, we also label people we never meet. Think of all the labels hung on our political figures.

The second problem with our rush to label is that we generalize experiences from the past to slap new labels on present situations. We stereotype new people based on our experiences with folks in our past; it's the easy way out.

We don't have time to get to know the new maintenance hand, so we rely on some superficial stereotypes that are readily available at first glance. He's in the maintenance department, so he must be like other maintenance folks at our plant. We might perceive him as combative and always in a bad mood because that has been our experience with other maintenance folks. We didn't take the time to get to know the new guy; he may be a great guy who coaches the pre-teen girls' soccer team and always brings in doughnuts to work for others to enjoy. Instead, we fit him into our stereotype of maintenance people. So, when he raises his hand to question a new safety rule we just pre-judge he's a troublemaker and probably don't listen to his otherwise-valid point.

We make assumptions, labels, based on limited data using our past experience to fit people into stereotypes. Our "data collection" is usually rushed and biased. From a limited set of interactions we create a sampling of findings, force it to conform to one of our labels for people, and then box the labeled person in that package. Once in that box we seek to confirm our label in any future interactions with that person. It's hard to leave the box once it's tied up in a tidy package.

To make matters worse, when our working memory capacity reaches overload, research shows that we suffer poorer impulse control. We are more likely to use the emotional core of our brain to make a decision when there is simply too much data to deal with (sound like a typical day at work?). This reduction in analytic judgment leads our labels to be biased and emotionally charged.

Just how accurate do you think your labels are? Certainly sometimes our labels may give us an accurate enough representation of reality. However, when we consider the human tendency to be biased in our judgments, well, we should take a second look at the confidence we put in our labels.

The Inaccuracy of Labels

Psychologically what is occurring when we label is that we commit what researchers call the "Fundamental Attribution Error." Here's how it works: an "attribution" is when you see someone behave and try to explain to yourself why that person did what you observed; you're attributing the behavior to a cause. Attributing assumptions about someone is an informed guess based on experience. Often we are bad at it. The problem is there is no such thing as mind-reading, so we end up guessing.

The "error" in the Fundamental Attribution Error is that we don't treat others like we treat ourselves. Consider your own attributions — explanations — when something bad happens to you. You're walking through your plant's fabrication unit chatting with a colleague and your thigh gets punched by a metal post extending out from a work table. Nice bruise you got there... why did that happen to you? What do you attribute as the cause of your new bruise? Most likely you will make an *external attribution*. You will look at the context of your behavior and blame the outcome on some external reason: "That lathe operator shouldn't have left that post in a position where someone walking by could run into it." You blamed an external source, in this case, someone else. And you probably labeled them. "That stupid lathe operator..." And, frankly, you protected your ego in the process by denying the bad outcome was due to your own incompetence or inattention.

Now what if we see the same thing happen to someone else? You see Joe from HR walking through the fabrication unit chatting with a colleague. He runs into the metal post, grimaces with pain, and grabs his thigh. You saw it coming, his head was turned talking to his colleague telling his silly HR joke and looking for a reaction. No eyes on path. So you make an attribution for his behavior. It's an "inside job." You probably blame the negative outcome of his behavior on some reason internal to Joe. "Idiot." What have you done? You have made an *internal attribution*. It was something inside Joe that caused him to get hurt.

Do you see the fallacy here? When something bad happens to you, you're likely to focus blame on the context of the situation to protect your ego. But you are less likely to be so generous to others. Instead, you're likely to blame the person with a label referencing an internal condition — such as idiocy.

Unless something good happens as a consequence of behavior… yup, then you turn your attribution error around.

This time you are walking through the fabrication unit with your colleague who happens to be the plant manager. You both are coming from a safety meeting. Your eyes are on path and you see the metal post extending from the work table. You stop to push the post fully on the table. The plant manager takes notice and praises you in the next staff meeting. What do you attribute this good outcome? Well, obviously, it is because you're attentive, smart, and a team player, labels you take pride in everyone knowing. Ahhh, an ego boost. You just made an *internal attribution* when something good happened to you.

Researchers theorize you make this mental error to protect your ego and self esteem. When bad outcomes occur you deflect blame to external factors, preserving your ego. When good outcomes happen, you attribute fate to positive internal factors, pumping up your ego.

People close to you, your friends and family, certainly don't escape your ability to make instant attributions. You give friends and family the benefit of the doubt when something bad happens to them. You are likely to blame the external situation for the negative outcome, just like you would if it happened to you. And when something awesome happens to them, you explain their awesomeness by giving them a positive label.

But how do you account for a stranger's behavior, the HR guy when something good happens to him. He's walking with his boss through the fabrication unit on the way from a safety meeting. He sees the metal post and repositions it onto the table. The boss is impressed and at the next staff meeting praises Joe for being attentive, smart, and a team player. But you sit in that meeting thinking, hell, Joe just came from a safety meeting where we were all shown pictures of housekeeping hazards and exhorted to be aware of our surroundings. Joe just happened to be lucky enough to come across such an obvious hazard when he was talking with the boss. You made an *external attribution* for Joe's behavior when something good happened to him. It was "luck" or because of the meeting. You didn't give him credit! It's a fundamental error we make — an illusion, an error of misinterpretation.

Now this all may seem quite cynical. Certainly there are people who push past their biases and deliver positive reinforcement to any and everyone. How do they push past their human tendency to bias and engage each other fairly and equally? They realize they cannot fix people; but they can change the environment through their behavior. They know by shaping the environment they can shape the behaviors they want to see in others. More on this in later chapters.

The Impotency of Attitudes

If we can just get our workers to have the right attitude, well, they will then choose to behave in ways that keep them safe. What a misconception! This makes the incorrect assumption that attitudes create behavior. But assuming someone has this-or-that attitude is, well, just another form of labeling.

Let's get this straight: Behaviors are NOT attitudes. They are much stronger, more concrete. You cannot see or hear an attitude. We only infer or attribute attitudes from watching someone's behavior.

The new maintenance guy asks a question about a new rule. We might look at that behavior and assume that he is arguing because he has an antagonistic attitude toward safety. We reason his antagonistic attitude toward safety causes him to behave combatively against any new safety rule. But this is all circular reasoning. You see his questioning as a manifestation of his bad attitude, but you base your attribution of his attitude on a label you gave him for asking these types of questions. He is merely asking a question, folks, and we get ourselves all wound up trying to fit his behavior into this mash up of assumptions and labels. In the end, you don't know what's happening in his head.

You can't see or hear beliefs, values, and other internal covert states of mind. You and I only think these states of mind exist because we experience them ourselves. It is as if someone inside our head is always talking to us, directing us, rewarding us at times and causing an uncomfortable dissonance at others.

Cognitive psychologists call this place, probably in our frontal lobes, "executive function." This executive function is a marvel of nature and it is what makes us humans, well, human. It allows us to draw on past experience to anticipate and plan beyond the moment. The executive function can help us push down our more basic animal impulses and delay reinforcement until this future beyond the moment arrives. It decides what to commit to memory to be used (or enjoyed) later. And, it is our memories that give our executive function a sense of "self"— we can experience our past in our present and we get the idea that we exist. We review our experiences from the past, both our external actions and our internal mental events, compare them to what's happening now, and build a theory of our "self" — who we are. A good thing, this executive function.

The reason we have such big brains compared to our fellow animals is that at one point in our ancestry we became social animals. We started teaming up with each other for a more successful hunt, to protect our families, to eventually grow food. Our brains grew to adapt to the human communication needed to compete with other animals, survive, and eventually take dominion over the world. It stands to reason that a big part of the evolved executive function is dedicated to human interaction.

When the executive function recognizes a pattern from self-talk, judgments, and emotional reactions it creates this theory about ourselves — what some call a "value," "belief" or "attitude." Yup, your executive function creates a label for you. Your executive function uses these self-labels to manage your experience, to filter stuff in and out of your consciousness. While highly efficient, this labeling process is not necessarily accurate. We exploit our personal bias to confirm our labels and beliefs as we go through the world. Confirmation is important in order to give us this illusion of a consistent world around us.

Some of us study our covert states of mind. What do I mean? Millions read self-help books and blogs. Some use therapy or meditation to do an internal inventory of self-talk and emotions to try to figure out why we behave the way we do. The scientific community calls these personal inspections "introspection." Introspection was popular in psychology until the 1900s when we learned that we are very biased and inaccurate observers of our internal world. Now research in psychology uses the scientific method of objective observations to avoid personal biases misinterpreting our thinking and conclusions.

Our attitudes don't always translate into behaviors. That's the bottom line. Similarly, attitudes of workers, supervisors and leaders don't always translate to the critical safety behaviors needed at work. Our values and intentions also don't always translate to actions.

Let's consider a critical piece of data from a safety culture survey administered to over 150,000 people worldwide. The following question was asked: "*Should employees caution coworkers when observing them perform at-risk behaviors?*" Over 90 percent of respondents agreed with this statement, reflecting their strong values around their need to look out for one another in an active way. Later in the survey we modified the question and asked: "*Are you willing to caution coworkers when observing them perform at-risk behaviors?*" Around 90 percent of respondents agreed that they have intentions to say something when they see something. The final question, appearing even later in the survey, asked the critical question: "*In the past month, have you cautioned coworkers when observing them perform at-risk behaviors?*" The percentage of respondents who said they actually acted on their values and intentions with the critical safety behavior dropped to 50 percent.

This is an important point: a gap definitely exists between our attitudes and our behaviors. We worry about folks with bad attitudes taking risks on the job, but even those with good intentions may fail to engage in behaviors that may keep themselves or others safe. To solve this riddle, let's force ourselves to confront our assumption that attitudes change behavior. Could the opposite be true? Could it be that behaviors change attitudes?

Behaviors change Attitudes, not the other way around

Consider this fundamental question: "*Do you think your way into a new way of acting?*" In other words, do your attitudes, beliefs, values, or intentions drive your behavior? Or is it the other way around: "*Do you act your way into a new way of thinking?*" Do you observe your behaviors and adapt your attitudes to be consistent with the way you act?

We are most functional in our lives when our attitudes align with our behavior. We are most happy at these times in our lives and more valuable to others. When our behaviors are incongruent with our attitudes we are less happy and functional. Emotionally we experience what psychologists call "dissonance." You can create dissonance in music when you put a minor note in a major chord. It creates a harsh sound that is irritating and you want it gone. In psychological terms, dissonance is that uncomfortable feeling when your internal voice seems to pester you for the inconsistency: "Why did I do that?"

Humans are motivated to get rid of this type of dissonance when their attitudes and behaviors don't jive. So something has to change. What changes then, our behavior or attitude?

Consider the young oil field worker who had gone through his HR and safety orientation when hired. After this practice in exhortation, his attitude may be to follow the rules because the job is dangerous and the rules are there to protect him. Then he finds himself out in the field where his supervisor and peers are skipping pressure checks to break down the fracking installation faster. In the heat of the moment he joins in and takes the short cuts with a knot in his belly, knowing his risky behavior is not what his attitude would direct him to do. When his crew finishes work within schedule they slap each other's backs and get a smile from the boss. There will be no reduction in their bonus for schedule overages.

So, what changes? Does the young roustabout's behavior change to be more consistent with his safety-focused attitude? Does he insist on doing the pressure checks and get further and further behind his peers' productivity?

Or does he continue taking the short cut too? To combat the dissonance between his original safety attitude and risky behavior, he fashions a different attitude: *"Faster is better when money is on the line."* His behavior changed his attitude. This new employee now looks at his own short cuts and concludes that productivity is priority one.

It may even explain how some folks get labeled CAVEmen. Green Hat comes out of the safety orientation having drunk the Kool-Aid. He values the safety systems he just learned would keep him out of harm's way on this dangerous job. He tells the trainers he appreciates their advice. But he goes into the field and starts taking the short cut, the easy, conventional way. He looks at his behavior and concludes he must not value safety as much as he thought. During his breaks he hears others complain about safety rules and the safety police who come around making trouble. Inevitably he begins to sample these sayings himself and gets laughs from his peers. He checks out his new behaviors and comes to a new attitude: this safety stuff is crap. This attitude only strengthens when he finds himself labeled as a "team player."

So that's what we do; we observe our own behaviors and try to rationalize to ourselves why we did it. This evolves into our attitude.

There is neuroscience evidence for this. If you've ever undergone an MRI scan you know it's uncomfortable because you're forced into an enclosed space. Van Veen did a now famous study where he had his subjects undergoing a scan tell the next participant that the MRI was a "pleasant experience." This produced dissonance because the scanning process is far from pleasant.

What Van Veen found in these MRI scans was that the dissonance activated the anterior cingulate cortex in the people who had to talk about how pleasant the experience is, but not in others who didn't. The anterior cingulate cortex is an area of your brain above your sinuses in the frontal lobe responsible for your executive functioning. Remember the executive function? It's the place where we form our attitudes.

Sure enough, these folks who told others that the experience was indeed "pleasant" ended up reporting that they actually did enjoy the scan. In contrast, others who did the scan but did not have to make false statements reported the scan as it was, unpleasant. Van Veen had found, in the anterior cingulate cortex, where attitude changes! The more the participants' attitude changes the more this cortex is fired.

Now get this: anterior cingulate cortex activity seems to increase when your behaviors cause errors in real life. Perhaps you find yourself taking short cuts on the job. Because the anterior cingulate cortex fires, your attitude begins to changes to be more in line with your behavior. Then, soon after, the left frontal cortex of your brain is activated. The left frontal cortex is the part of the brain that reduces anger. Get it? You reduce dissonance when you change your attitude.

Neuroscience confirms the relationship between behavior and attitudes:

1. You behave in ways inconsistent with your attitude →

    2. This creates dissonance/anger →

        3. Activity in the anterior cingulate cortex increases →

            4. You experience an attitude change →

                5. Activity in the left Frontal cortex increases →

                    6. Your dissonance and anger reduces →

                        7. All is cool again.

Folks, this is a game changer! Labels take us down a rabbit hole. We try again and again to change attitudes through labeling exhortations. Nothing changes and we remain frustrated.

This gives us hope! You can change the attitude by changing behavior. Find a way to get your people to practice the behaviors that exemplify the attitudes you want to build. And as they engage in these behaviors they will see their performance and conclude it must be indicative of their attitude. Poof — double whammy! Behavior and attitude change.

> You change attitudes by changing behavior. You act your way into a new way of thinking, not the other way around.

This is the heart of behavioral safety. The challenge is to get your people to practice the behaviors consistent with the behavioral safety program. In your training, have employees practice observing analyzing at-risk behaviors and providing feedback to peers. Then, on the job, go out with them and have them practice the same behaviors. First have them observe and coach you, Next, accompany workers as they observe and coach someone else. Keep on keeping on until your people are fluent and comfortable with the process. The more they have supervised practice of the pro-safety behaviors the better. At one point they will start observing their own behavior in relation to coaching peers and supporting the BBS program. They will then experience an attitude change: *"I've been talking with my buddies about how to do their job safer, I must buy in to this safety thing."* It works! Seriously, try it!

This is why you want to have many different employees present a safety message during the beginning-of-shift toolbox talks or other safety meetings. You'll encourage everyone, even the CAVEman, to say something about safety. Giving them easy and frequent opportunities to behave in a pro-safety way will change their attitude bit by bit.

This is why employee engagement in safety is such a powerful thing! In addition to getting good ideas from the folks who are out there experiencing the hazards, you get everyone to frequently behave in ways that will result in pro-safety attitude change. And THEN you've enhanced your safety culture.

DYSFUNCTIONAL PRACTICE: RUSHING TO JUDGE

Labeling can be a catharsis when emotions are high, but we will remain frustrated because you can't fix a label. Saying that someone has the wrong attitude is yet another impotent label.

Labels are mental shortcuts performed by your brain. They are stereotypes based on generalizations and limited analytic judgment. These judgments are generally inaccurate due to our human biases of attribution leading to misinterpretations.

You can't change attitudes through exhortation. You change attitudes by changing behavior. You act your way into a new way of thinking, not the other way around.

Find small ways for your employees to promote safety. They will observe their own behavior and experience an attitude change: "I've been talking about safety to my peers, I must buy in to safety."

CHAPTER 4:

Fishing for Faults

A MANAGER HAD BEEN STUCK IN HIS OFFICE completing still more paperwork. Today his crew was changing a motor in plant #7 and he knew this was a high-profile event due to its process safety implications. They were nearing the end of the year and he certainly didn't want any process safety incidents on his record, and he couldn't afford another injury. Lord knows there are a lot of strains, bangs, and burns you can get working that motor. He decided to leave the rest of the emails unattended so he could go out and check if his guys were doing everything correctly to avoid injury. Sure enough, when he got to the plant three guys were finishing their work and he saw that one of them didn't have his face shield down as they tested for leaks with the lines activated. The manager caught the worker with an apparent violation. This guy's day was about to get a lot worse.

The manager had gone on a fishing trip for at-risk behavior. And he "hooked" one of his crew doing "wrong." He found what he was looking for — at-risk behavior — and administered discipline, based on this single data point.

He didn't consider all the safe behaviors he overlooked. Indeed, the crew had confirmed the LOTO tags before unwiring, made sure they had at least three people to lift the motor, and used proper carts and ladders throughout the process. They were even doing the leak test to avoid a future process safety incident, a step a lot of crews skip or forget. As they were running the motor to test performance levels one guy took a break to get a drink to fight fatigue. He lifted his face shield to drink and forgot to drop it back as he returned to the job. This whole flow of safe behaviors was ignored. The manager only targeted the face shield violation and wrote up one of the team. Did he show that he valued the safe work the team had done?

No. He swooped in from nowhere, like a spying drone. He got angry as he scolded the young man who forgot his face shield. As for the rest of the team, he came off as a grump. Nothing positive to say. He scared the young man and made him feel useless. Worse, consider the longer term implications if this manager had a habit of "spying." Do you think the young man or his fellow laborers would want to interact about safety with this manager in the future? What if they are concerned about the hazards when doing a future motor change? Do you think they would feel comfortable reporting a near miss to him? He shut down everyone — and made them more likely to hide their safety errors. This erodes a safety culture — and the damage is inflicted using but a single data point.

But let's not label and blame the manager. Just like any human, his behavior was shaped over time. He had been molded to favor aversive tactics such as scolding, threats, and discipline over more positive ones such as praise. And his approach was based on a very limited sampling — a single data point, a single incident.

Everything Varies

Early in my career, I worked closely with industrial engineers, a nice bunch with the world-view that everything can be designed to run smoothly and safely. We had formed a company to help organizations improve their performance and we considered ourselves on the cutting edge blending engineering and psychology. Incidentally, when we built the behavioral safety processes you know today, this blend of engineering and psychology helped us design the systems that supported its success. Needless to say, interacting with these folks shaped my approach to safety profoundly.

We were a part of the quality revolution of the 1990s led by our guru Dr. W. Edwards Deming. I had attended Deming's workshops three times, enough to pound in my head many of his mantras: *"We must understand variation;" "Whenever there is fear, you get the wrong figures;" "Manage the cause, not the results."*

Deming was a statistician who saw the world in terms of variance. Psychologists also view the world by seeing variance and looking for its sources. We don't look at single data points at a single point in time to determine our worldview. Instead, we look at differences. We recognize that there are differences across and within people. Different people generate different levels of performance. And, a single person over time will perform at different levels. This is the same for teams as well as operational performance around productivity, quality, and, of course, safety.

Deming taught us to understand the sources of this variance in order to reduce it and improve performance. When viewing injury data such as incident rates and behavioral observation data, we don't look at this quarter or this year's number and see it as an absolute description of safety performance — because it isn't. A single quarter's number is an aggregate based on certain definitions, across a determined time period, and dependent on good reporting. Actually, it's <u>very</u> dependent on good reporting and good reporting is often suspect. When you look at a single data point like a quarterly report, you can't tease out the unreliability that can come from humans who make errors.

Instead, look for variation across time, variation across work units, comparisons to industry norms, and the like. I promise you that quite interesting and actionable conclusions can be drawn from otherwise hidden realities within this variance.

Similarly, many in the safety world look to an investigation for answers when someone gets injured. All well and good, but we also make the mistake of searching for absolutes. When we wait for the investigations to draw a single conclusion, we have neglected the dozens of stories, the dozens of variations in human behavior that, if measured, would have revealed a basis for action *before the injury*. A good measurement system can save a world of hurt... literally. This is one of the reasons why high levels of observations in behavioral safety systems are related to reductions in injuries in study after study. When observations go up, injuries go down. One reason for this, on top of the peer-to-peer coaching, is that high numbers of observation allow us to trend the variance and find the risks that could lead to injury.

If you don't understand and look for variation, your limited view of the world blinds you to risk. Deming said that one of the greatest mistakes managers make is "single data-point management." Unfortunately, in the safety world I see too many single data-point managers.

Fishing for Violations

My son loves to fish. He and I are different. I like to sit out in nature pondering random thoughts as I watch light dance across the water. I don't care if I catch anything. He prefers actually baiting and hooking the fish. We go to the lake, he throws out his line, and waits to reel in that one fish of the unseen thousands.

This type of fishing reminds me of single data-point management. A manager or supervisor (perhaps even you) is responsible for performance on measures consisting of outcome data (such as injuries), instrumentation data (from machines or via other forms of technology) and the like. You spend your work day looking for the kinds of errors that can hurt these numbers. You don't want to wait until an incident happens, because it would suck for you and your numbers. Instead, you engage in walk-arounds (when you're not mired in email) to find errors so you can react to them before they conspire to create a negative outcome (such as an injury). These walk-arounds are like fishing trips. You are searching for violations of rules. You've got your line out and are trolling for rule-breaking behavior.

Safety management often resembles blind fishing. You don't pay attention to thousands of safe behaviors, and, believe me, the vast, vast majority of behaviors out there are safe. Instead, we just hunt for violations. We almost feel if we don't catch something, it isn't a successful walk-around. So we continue looking for that singular instance in which a worker's behavior gives us what we think is a clear danger signal. Then we yank on the line to attempt to hook the violation.

Once, my sons and I went fishing with a guide on a chilly day in the mangrove swamps in the Florida Keys. The fish were not biting because it was so cold. The guide wanted my young sons to score some catches so he threw "chum" into the water (something like candy for fish) to draw the fish to us. Fortunately for our vacation, the boys did catch a couple of small hungry fish.

Managers and supervisors often are scrutinized in their safety role. It's easy. Someone gets hurt and recordable incidents spike. The manager or supervisor is put on the spot, plain and simple. Logic, according to Heinrich, is that these recordables are happening because there has been an increase in at-risk behavior. Everyone is put on notice. Find it. Stop it. This directive is management's version of "chum." Got to do something.

If a manager or supervisor finds people taking risks they feel they've done a good job. They hoist up their fish proudly, *"Look what I caught,"* and get to tell their tall tale of how they snared such a big fish. The "fisherman" may even feign exasperation of the at-risk behavior, but really they're excited to tell the tale. The story of the stupid employee. *"Look at my fish!"* Colleagues comment on how large a fish was caught. *"Oh yeah, nice fish."*

Rarely if ever does anyone tell stories about finding an employee managing hazards around them using safe behaviors. Good news doesn't travel far. The absence of a guy doing something careless, stupid, is not a good story. We don't get to use those negative labels.

Fish stories only encourage managers and supervisors to troll for safety violations. They want their own story! Chum is out and we are seeking to catch even the smallest fish. As more trolling takes place, even the smallest violations get caught, perhaps a young man with his face shield up as he was walking back to a job after a break. Success! We stopped a safety violation.

BUT… these apparent successes are another illusion based on single data-point management; a misguided practice.

The illusion makes you think you are doing something productive to promote safety. In fact you're actually unintentionally promoting injuries; and diminishing your managerial skills in the process. And… you become a grumpus. It happens and you probably are not even aware of it.

Punishing Praise

Remember when you were first promoted to a managerial job or were given that space on the employee safety committee? You were excited and a little nervous. You now had clear responsibility for other people, folks just like yourself. You probably didn't start your new job thinking, *"I'm going to be pissed off all the time and scold employees."* You probably approached your assignment thinking, *"I'm going to be THAT boss; the one folks like and want around, the boss who makes you feel good with praise."* Admit it, that's how you started.

But over time you built up the illusion that praise does not work. Instead, by chumming the waters during your fishing trips for violations, you turned into a scolding and grumpy supervisor. Here's how it happened.

The reality is simple: each of your employees has good moments and bad moments. You do too. All of us have moments of good safety performance where we make conscious efforts to keep ourselves and others safe. At other times we may have moments when we take risks, intentionally or unconsciously. Safety-related behaviors — good and bad —

are happening all the time. And over time, most employees have average days where performance varies across little incidents of safe and at-risk behaviors. For the most part we end the day safe and productive.

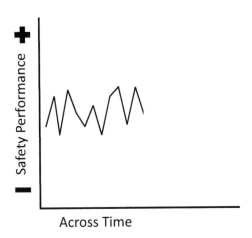

Across Time

When we troll for rule violations, we fail to pay attention to this variance. We overlook the fact that the employee has been in the act of behaving all the time, across time. Instead, we end up trolling for isolated, individual behaviors that we can catch.

Since you started out aspiring to be the positive boss, you probably first started trolling for "good" safe behaviors. What you were most likely to notice were the outliers in performance, when your employees did something outside the norm. Perhaps you noticed a particular employee do something exceptional to enhance safety.

Consider this example. Tired of waiting for an engineered fix, Sam built a guard on a mixer that had worn down and presented a hazard. Sam complained about the hazard for a month and finally decided to do something. He talked with friends in fabrication who whipped up a serviceable guard that he could install at the beginning of the next shift.

You saw Sam installing the newly fabricated guard and praised him for taking initiative. Perhaps you even recognized his effort in front of his team at the next toolbox meeting. *"Hey folks, I want to take a moment to recognize Sam. Sam saw that the guard had worn off the mixing unit and he took initiative to do something about it. He took the old guard to the fabrication building and had them create a new one. As he installed it I told him that his actions probably kept someone from having their hand slip into the unit. I hope the rest of you take the same initiative as Sam when you see something wrong. Good job Sam!"*

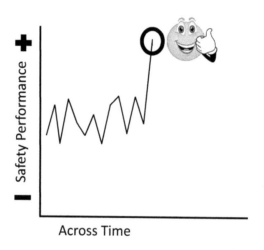

Across Time

Don't misunderstand me here. Good management skills were exhibited by praising Sam. The praise identified the specific safe behavior and pointed out the positive consequence resulting from the behavior. Praise is good and the more praise that's given the easier it becomes. Unfortunately, praising behavior is unlikely to last. What happens next creates an illusion that praise doesn't work. If you don't think praise works you stop doing it.

Let's return to that single data point. Sam's exceptional performance was an outlier. He typically did not go around fixing machinery on a daily basis. He just fixed his machine in this instance because he was fed up. It was out of his norm. Prior to that, Sam's behavior varied in small ways that at times helped him be a little safer in some instances, and perhaps a bit more at-risk at other times. This is how Sam will act in the future as well.

Sam's behavior when he fixed a guard was "exceptional" so, by definition, it was out of his norm. When any of us have an exceptional moment we rarely follow it up consistently with continued exceptionality (unless we ourselves are exceptional… but I doubt that).

I'm a relatively bad golfer. This is to say my typical shot is not good. I'm happy when my slice does not veer off into the woods or my chip does not sail over the green. Like Sam, my performance varies around some average. Some shots are better than others and some, um, let's just say are not up to par. But then I experience those moments when I hit the little white ball just right. My body releases its coil smoothly as the club swings through the ball sending it straight and true, landing just one foot from the hole. I feel great. My friends heap praise on me for my exceptional shot.

What happens next? Do I continue to play exceptional and have the best round of my career? More likely I regress back to my typical performance and dig up a chunk of earth with my 7-iron, failing to reach the green on the next fairway. We regress to the norm of our behavior. It is a fundamental principle of human performance.

This pattern reverberates through your life. Your performance continually bounces up and down in small ways. You'll have an extraordinary bounce in performance every now and then, giving you hope that things are looking up. But then nothing significant is sustained so you regress back to your norm, probably disappointing yourself in the process. Similarly, your workers' safety performance will bounce up and down in small ways as days and weeks pass. Every now and then their behavior will have an extraordinary impact on their own safety or the safety of others. Most of the time, no one is there to see it.

But, in our example, you happened to come upon Sam's extraordinary performance when he took the initiative to switch out the worn guard. You went to great lengths to praise Sam in front of his peers, probably embarrassing him in the process. You're proud. Now you're expecting great things from Sam.

However, Sam's performance is going to regress back to his norm, just like my golf game. During the next shift, you're excited to go out into the unit again to see what something exceptional Sam has in store for you now. You go to his work area and quickly notice that he is wearing all of his PPE and the new guard is indeed dropped into place to separate the mixing blades from his hands. However, Sam has yet to clean up the tools he used to install the new guard. The clamps, drills, bits, screws are still scattered on the floor behind him. In fact, he nearly trips on the old guard as he steps away from his machine to respond to your greeting. Predictably and unintentionally, Sam regressed back to his norm of performance swinging between small variations of safe and at-risk behavior.

Ah, but you fall prey to the illusion. Yesterday you were proud of Sam and praised him publicly. Today you observe that Sam's safety performance has dropped; he hasn't done some basic housekeeping.

You think to yourself: *"I just praised Sam and now he's doing something stupid."* You may even go so far to think: *"He got all pumped up from the praise and seems to think that he doesn't have to do basic housekeeping any longer."*

You associate the drop in his safety performance to the praise he received the day before. You begin to assume that this praise thing does not work. In fact, praise ends up making people perform worse — more unsafely.

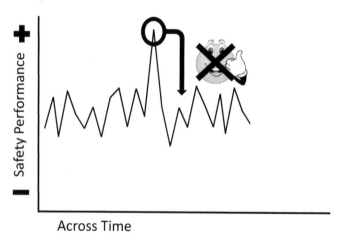

Across Time

But this assumption is another illusion. It was not your praise that caused the drop in performance. It happened naturally. It was bound to happen. It's a fundamental principle of human performance.

We often don't see this natural variation because we're caught up in single data-point management. We continue to build on the illusion that praise has no impact as we go through this scenario a couple times. Every time we praise one of our employees for doing something extraordinary they seem to pay us back with a slip in performance (the illusion). Over time, our praising gets punished and we get shaped to avoid praising (see chart). And that's too bad, because our employees deserve praise for safe behavior.

So you rarely praise now. But how did you turn completely into a grumpus?

Reinforcing Scolding

As you become shaped, honed by experience not to praise, you fall prey to yet another illusion, the false impression that scolding works. On another walk-around you come across Patricia working on her loom. Typically, Patricia seems to work safely. However, on this day she removed the guard at the bottom where the fabric was rolled into the conveyor. You intervene. You are upset and disappointed.

You scold Patricia and she tries to explain that the guard had worn and kept slipping into the roller, making her stop production to reset. You warn her that the guards were there for a reason and if her hand slipped on the loom and dropped into the roller it could be crushed. You raise your voice so other seamstresses will hear as you reprimand Patricia, hoping they will avoid making the same mistake. You finish up by firmly stating that the rules require Patricia to stop work and notify you if any safety equipment was not working. She didn't and now she is in trouble.

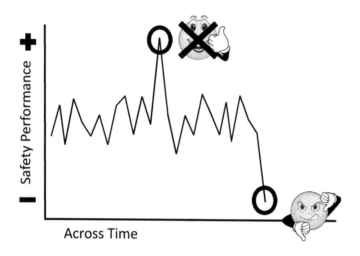

After this interaction you might feel bad for Patricia. You laid it on thicker than you should have. Certainly Patricia did not respond in a chipper mood. But, you reason, it was for a good cause because the "coaching" may have saved her and others from hurt and handicap.

Still, you probably resolve to handle it differently next time.

The next shift rolls around and you intend to mend some fences by asking about non-work stuff like the local charity you know Patricia is passionate about. When you approach the looms Patricia isn't at her post. Did your scolding so upset her that she was taking longer breaks or simply finding ways to avoid you? You turn to another seamstress to ask about Patricia and spot her on the other side of the unit. She is sweeping up the fiber residue from the looms and conveyers, a house-keeping behavior that reduces the chance of slipping in an area where a lot of folks walk.

Here is where the second illusion may hit home. You may perceive: *"I just scolded her for at-risk behavior yesterday. Look what happened today, her safety performance increased. This scolding thing works! Not only is she less likely to disable her guard, it looks like she is stepping up in other ways."*

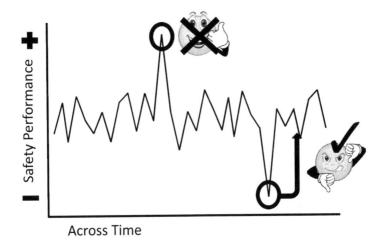

Again you make use of a single data point to draw an incorrect assumption about Patricia's intentions. You never noticed that the loom unit floors always were clean and uncluttered. Sweeping was one of the small safety-oriented behaviors that Patricia did on and off as part of her routine, as part of the norm of behaviors, both safe and at-risk, that made up her work life. But you don't consider the safety behaviors you see now are simply an extension of her norm. Instead you hold on to the illusion that your scolding influenced her to engage in more safety-centric behaviors... dare you say, you "caused it"?

This scenario only need happen a couple times and you get reinforced for scolding, reprimanding, and issuing threats of discipline. In the future you become more likely to scold.

But this is a superstition. It's the type of superstition that afflicts baseball managers who walk out to talk to their pitcher; they always make sure they avoid stepping on the base line for fear of causing a home run on the next pitch. In behavior science we call superstition "adventitious reinforcement." The definition of adventitious is instructive: "*happening or carried on according to chance rather than design or inherent nature* (thanks Google)." It was by chance that the manager happened to step on the base line in the past right before his pitcher gave up a game-winning home run. And it was a chance happening that when he avoided the line the pitcher then struck out the star batter. The chalk line has nothing to do with the pitcher's performance or the game outcome. Nor does your one-time single data-point praising or scolding have any lasting impact on your employee's safety performance. Still, you are human and as a human you form attributions quickly and errantly, based on biases. The result? You form labels and assumptions that sometimes do not really exist.

Many of us begin our careers with the intent of being the positive boss who lifts employees up so they can succeed at work. Instead a different management style is created by an insidious superstition that slowly, at first, is shaped by adventitious reinforcement. This increases our use of negative practices like scolding and discipline. Eventually management behavior becomes more punitive. Shaping is like that. Negative comments turn into scolding, scolding to reprimanding, reprimanding to threats of discipline, threats to administering discipline.

Then, to maximize the effect we go fishing, looking for opportunities to use unpleasant consequences. We're under the illusion that they work. We get good at fishing, throwing out that line, trying to catch bad behavior. When we catch one, we're a bit excited (if we're honest with ourselves) and show others our prize catch. We know what to do when we catch one, we threaten discipline, we do discipline. This can shape any of us into quite the grumpy dude. When we're out there fishing for risks we fail to see the plethora, the overwhelming majority, of safe behaviors taking place. We fail to see the variation that exists, the very variation that can help us solve problems and create a safer workplace. Even worse, we're not stopping injuries.

When we fish for risks we fail to see the plethora of safe behaviors taking place. We fail to see the variation that can help us solve problems and create a safer workplace.

To make matters worse, managers' and supervisors' performance is evaluated based on the number of injuries (minor and more severe) in their unit. It's part of the scorecard that links to evaluations and pay increases. This type of scoring begets trolling, looking for violations.

Thinking that this will improve the numbers.

The fault of most measurement systems is they only count something when there is an incident. This includes many measures in our safety management systems: Injury rates, near miss/first aids, equipment damages, safety violations are typical examples. When we use these measures no information is good information because a bad occurrence has not been detected. Think about it. The status quo, what is happening most of the time, is zero incidents. If you average 24 incidents a year that actually means that you have zero incidents for two weeks at a time! It's the norm, the status quo. Of course this way of looking at injury rates is fallacy because zero incidents, no matter how long the streak goes, do not mean that risks that can eventually hurt someone are being avoided by your employees. Risks are still being taken. But relying on incident rates is a kind of false security. The fact is we don't have the measures to find and analyze the risks that are out there.

Instead of measures that show variation, measures such as injury rates and violations are binary. They either happen or they don't — ones and zeros, folks. Most of the time we are measuring a "zero" day after day, building complacency. Our concerted efforts only kick in when there is a "one," when there is an incident. Zero, zero, zero, rule violation; we then swoop in, investigate, mitigate, label someone stupid, and we are back to zero, zero, zero. Are all these zeros a reflection of reality?

Don't be fooled by this illusion. Instead look for variation, discover its source, and manage it. Better fisher folk than I use sonar in their boats. Sonar bounces sound waves down toward the lake bottom. Schools of fish reflect this wave back to the sensors and appear on the sonar screen, giving you a good idea of where fishing may be productive. Modern sonar can locate size and composition for individual fish by bouncing sound waves up to 40 times a second. Fisher folk have even figured out that the speed of the sonar pulse (sound) is affected not only by depth but by water salinity (which is a constant on a lake) and temperature. Add a temperature gauge and you can now tell the distance of the fish from the boat. Those of you in oil exploration know that sonar has become so advanced that it can detect not only the geography of the ocean floor but also gaseous seeping out of promising wells. We will do all this sophisticated measuring for pleasure fishing yet we leave our safety measurement in the hands of ones and zeros.

A good measurement system scans your operations objectively, looking for pockets of variation that may reflect hazards and risks. When you find this variance, use your problem-solving tools to cast your net over the potential problem and solve it... before harm results.

But... you can only look at variation and its sources if employees are participating in measurement through programs such as behavioral safety and other types of reporting. Outcome data such as injury rates are not sufficiently sensitive or granular — not specific enough. Nor are your own walk-arounds, because they probably reflect your personal biases. What you find is influenced by your mere presence.

Instead, turn to your employees who are able to provide the insights into the variance you want to uncover. They know the sources of variance; they can collect those data in a no-name/no-blame system of the type found to be successful in behavioral safety; and they can help reduce that variance.

And instead of counting the uncommon occurrences of incidents in binary fashion, you can count up occurrences of reporting, participation, suggestions, and actions taken based on the insights of employees empowered to participate in your safety program.

After all, isn't having the fish just jump in the boat (Google this!) a fisherman's dream?

DYSFUNCTIONAL PRACTICE:
FISHING FOR FAULTS

Managers are shaped to look for faults and favor aversive tactics such as scolding, threats, and discipline. They go fishing, trying to find at-risk behavior based on single data points and miss the behavioral variance that is the real source of risk.

When we fish for risks we fail to see the plethora of safe behaviors taking place. We fail to see the variation that can help us solve problems and create a safer workplace.

Instead of showing variation, measures such as injury rates and violations are binary. Recording a "zero" day after day builds complacency.

A good measurement system scans your operations objectively, looking for pockets of variation that may reflect hazards and risks.

Find variance in occurrences of reporting, participation, suggestions, and actions taken based on the insights of employees empowered to participate in your safety program.

CHAPTER 5:

The Fear Response

FISHING EXPEDITIONS — TROLLING FOR VIOLATIONS — frighten employees. Think about it from the employees' perspective. When they see a fishing expedition coming their way, they anticipate something negative will happen. When they are being observed, they worry it will be used against them. Nothing positive there!

In this chapter I want to talk about fear in the workplace, specifically as it relates to safety. To do this I need to go into a bit of how our brains work — neuroscience, which is a hot topic in psychology — and safety — today.

Our body is equipped with automatic protective wiring that has been part of our animal selves since before we were endowed with higher reasoning from an enlarged frontal cortex. Our body automatically and continuously reacts to different stimuli around us (and in us). Reactions can be simple like temperature regulation to the much more complex, like falling in love. This system is what keeps our body chemistry balanced so it can work optimally as we go through life.

All of this works in the underside of our brain without us knowing. Put your hand at the base of your skull right where your neck connects and you'll find where this happens. We are talking about the structures of the brainstem and cerebellum. Don't worry, there will not be a test on this later, but to appreciate how our body reacts automatically to workplace situations we should understand physical functioning.

When we work hard at our jobs our body adjusts by sending sugars and oxygen to our muscles and brain for optimal performance. We only become aware of it when there are imbalances that demand our attention. This occurs when we get fatigued for example. Our body temperature may get abnormally high evaporating our fluids. Our blood sugars may deplete and lactic acids build up causing our muscles cramp. Oxygen in our blood decreases and our thoughts get fuzzy. Only then do we notice and act. We take a break and drink some water (and perhaps some salt). The trick is to teach workers to recognize these signs early, before they impact body performance and judgment and put them at-risk without knowing it.

Fatigue is a body's slow reaction to work. We also have lightning quick automatic reactions in our reflexes. I was at a food distribution center in the midwestern U.S. where they had a spike in injuries associated with a major increase in volume due to consolidation of operations after a merger. The volume of cases going through the warehouse tripled and the company had to double its staff (and add a lot of overtime) to deal with it. Most of the injuries were among new, mostly young and inexperienced new hires. While I was there a forklift was replenishing selectors by pulling full pallets from three-story racks. A young forklift operator, still on a probationary hire, turned into a metal beam spanning two sets of racks and knocked the beam off its bracings. The five-foot beam smashed into the ground three stories below with a sonic clash. My body jumped immediately and automatically.

We ran to the site of the incident where we found two ashen-faced individuals. One was the young man who was startled by what he had done. The other was a young lady splayed on the floor about five feet from the fallen beam, clipboard another five feet away. We helped her up and after a couple moments she started talking. She remembered what happened but was unsure how she ended up on the floor. he was at the end of the row completing her inventory looking at a set of skew numbers. In her peripheral vision, "the corner of her eye," she experienced something coming at her. She didn't have time to perceive what the object was. Her reflexes reacted before the rest of her brain could completely perceive the falling object. The next thing she knew her body was plunging to the floor, out of the path of the falling beam, quickly accompanied by a surge of fear. This all happened so fast that she only knew what happened after she was on the floor. Oddly, she felt like she jumped away on purpose but, in reality, our bodies react automatically and only afterward do we interpret what happened (remember this important point for later).

Consider hazards your workers are exposed to all day, every day. When I visit your worksites these hazards are new to me. I experience a fear response when I ride down into an open mine on a haul truck or when I'm a couple feet from a flaming cauldron of hell. I have a flight reaction because there are things that can kill or maim me. There I am shaking in my steel toes while my hosts and the workers doing their jobs are calm as cucumbers. I'm reminded of the famous photograph taken in 1932 of iron workers building a skyscraper casually sitting on an I-beam far above the Manhattan skyline eating lunch.

Workers' bodies have habituated to these environments. Habituation is when you experience lower and lower levels of physiological and emotional response as you come in contact with a frequently repeated hazard or other scary stimulus. If you go day-after-day interacting with a hazard without injury or a scary event the body's response lessens, as does the perception of fear. In fact, some level of habituation may be necessary for workers in high-hazard jobs to complete their tasks. I remember once being frozen with fear on the top of a 20-foot ladder while hiking a high mountain. My fear response exposed me to greater risks of falling with each passing second. If the ironworkers toiling at great heights always reacted with trembling fear they could not be productive and probably would put themselves greater at risk traversing around with a tense body. To work around hazards we need to habituate so we are not encumbered by the fear response.

However, a little bit of fear around hazards is necessary. It keeps us alert and primed for emergency. A tad of fear makes us more aware of our behaviors and in tune with the potential severe consequences that could happen. Unfortunately, we can't consciously regulate habituation to make it useful. It is another automatic process. And habituation can be dangerous. It diminishes fear to the point we put ourselves at risk.

Fatigue and reflexes are unlearned automatic reactions of our body. Some of our reactions are learned over time. We learn through experience how to react to social interactions that often are laden with emotion. We learn to deal with those emotions, not always in the most positive way, but we learn to respond.

Emotions and the Chicken or the Egg Question

How we react to labeling, fishing expeditions, and even praise at work involves emotions. These are in fact the same complex, automatic responses as before, but emotions get associated with people (like the boss), places (like the training room) or things (like an inspection sheet) as a result of experience.

Fear is an emotion. Emotions can overwhelm us, enlighten us, or leave us bored. It's commonly believed that emotions lead to the bodily responses you experience. You feel sorrow and then your belly hurts. You feel happy and your lips turn up into a smile. But guess what, this is yet another illusion. Psychological research indicates that the sequence of events is the other way around. Emotions are just your brain's explanation for the automatic bodily responses you experience. Something happens to us. Our body responds first. Only then does our mind (the executive center) interpret how our body feels and we call it an emotion.

Someone makes a funny face and we laugh. Think about it. Did you actually see the face, think it was funny first and then decide to smile and laugh? No way, it happened too fast and without thinking. Instead, someone makes a funny face and automatically our face tenses and our diaphragm convulses slightly with a sharp series of exhales making a laughing sound. We get a rush of endorphins in the pleasure zone of our brain. Soon after these automatic series of reactions play out, your mind, having observed all this, concludes, "That was funny, I must be amused." Body reaction first, emotion second.

This seems counterintuitive. We believe we are masters of our body movements. But this is a trick our brain plays on us. Decades of research shows we tend to react first and think later. Try it out; you can manufacture your emotions with this little insight. Spend the next ten minutes with a smile on your face. You'll soon find yourself "happy." It works even better if you are around other people. Now consider this: many fishing managers walk around frowning. They are fishing for problems. Is it any wonder why they find themselves grumpy? This is not a pleasant experience.

Fear is an emotion that contorts us. Our body responds and our mind interprets. Our body learns though experience to associate its automatic responses with the people, places and things that are present in the moment when they happen. If you experience a fear response a number of times when your boss is present, your body will automatically react this way in her presence in the future… and you interpret this as "fear."

I recall driving three hours over the South African escarpment westward out of Johannesburg to visit a mining construction site. The mine had recently rolled out its behavioral safety system, brand new in this country, and the site was proud of the initial adoption by the workforce. The team at the construction site claimed to have experienced a change in culture. I was there to investigate this change… from what? … to what? The first question was answered immediately as I drove onto the site. There in front of me, painted in huge letters on the water tower, was the phrase: "DON'T FEAR SAFETY."

How do people get to a point where they fear safety? After all, safety processes are not hazards. They protect you when you have 300-foot falls or flames licking at you. How can something like a checklist or an SOP or a safety manager create fear?

Is this just a problem in South Africa where the slimmest of safety violations can immediately get you fired and replaced by thousands waiting for your job? Or can it also be an issue at plants with the most progressive safety professionals?

Let's return to how our body learns to automatically respond to familiar contexts around us. Then let's look at how this explains the fear typically associated with safety programs and the dysfunctional effect is has. If we can understand fear in the workplace we can counteract it and strengthen our safety culture in the process.

Fear is not for Sissies

As I explained, fear is an automatic bodily reaction. We all experience it. It's part of our body's protective mechanisms. Fear is a solid, dependable defense against a variety of "offenses" or threats. We need fear. But here's the key: what we do with our fear distinguishes a hero from a coward. Our heroes experience fear — ask soldiers in combat. But they handle it differently from civilians. You heroes reading this know this well.

One caveat: heroes experience fear unless they have an antisocial personality disorder. But then they are unlikely to be a hero. Sociopathology is, in part, characterized by a lack of a fear response. Criminals diagnosed with antisocial personality disorder have 30 percent lower production of stress hormones when confronted with a stressful situation. Kind of convenient when you're going to rob a house. These folks, especially murderers, have significantly less activity in their frontal lobes, the area that helps us reason our way through stressful situations. In fact, repeat offenders have been found to have 11 percent less brain matter in their frontal lobes. Still, I want to emphasize that fear is good — if it is heroically directed at the right thing.

However, most of us don't appropriately manage the fear response. We feel distressed when it hits, become less rational, and do whatever we can to escape it. In fact, once we experience it we do whatever we can to avoid coming in contact with fear again. Fear positions our body to be on alert, ready for threats. This can be stressful. Not comfortable. We're tight, tensed up.

What happens when you feel stressed out? The automatic response system we've been talking about in this chapter is called the sympathetic nervous system (it is "sympathetic" to the strong stimuli around us). This system arouses the body to fight or flee in the face of threats. The manager nearly falling from the step-ladder experienced this, as did all of us at the warehouse when the beam crashed. Nothing even needs to actually happen, just being near hazards can set it off. I experienced the same driving down into that mine.

When a threatening stimulus occurs — perhaps a hazard, perhaps an angry boss — the sympathetic nervous system fires up your adrenal gland to release hormones that supercharge your body. Your liver releases an abundance of sugars to power muscles. Your heart rate accelerates to deliver oxygen to these muscles. Your pupils dilate to improve vision. You're ready to fight — or flee if it's a tiger or a psychopath.

Having our bodies constantly in this state of readiness harms your health. Feeling distressed all the time causes hypertension and, to make matters worse, your sympathetic nervous system turns off your digestive system (ever have diarrhea after a stressful week?). Distress is dangerous if it is associated with your work every day. We need an alternative to this potential harm.

Normally, when we are relaxed our body is actually hard at work. Another part of our automatic response system is called the parasympathetic nervous system. The parasympathetic nervous system directs our body to conserve its resources and focuses on digesting our food and storing energy. While our digestive systems are working our heart rate slows, muscles relax, and our breath is drawn at a nice deep pace. We may even feel a slight euphoria that is associated with what we interpret as "relaxation."

Yes, relaxation is an automatic response! To get there you have to turn off the fear system and "get beyond" it. "Para" means to get beyond. You can turn on your parasympathetic nervous system whenever you want. It is easy and if you don't know how, you should learn. This state of relaxation is very helpful and healthy for you. You can use it to counteract fear responses when they become counterproductive. Get good at it and turn on the parasympathetic to improve your health as you practice.

Ready? Find a comfortable spot in your chair. Stare at one point on the wall, eyes slightly lowered. Now take three breaths. One, draw it in and on the slow exhale let your shoulders drop. Notice how much they dropped? Wow, you had a lot of tension going on there. Second breath, in, slow exhale out, this time letting your body sink heavily into your chair. Be a big heavy lump. Finally, third deep breath, and notice on the exhale how you heavy body feels a bit numb. There, you just "Para-ed." Practice this exercise, a peaceful sensation with a tad of, shall we say, happiness.

I want you to learn this feeling because you can generate it any time you want. The more you practice the better you'll get at finding it, and the more available it will be in times of need.

What are those times of need? How about when you have your annual review and your numbers don't look good? How about when there is tension on the worksite when a CAVEman gets antagonistic? My prescription is to write down ten events that stress you out. I bet just writing them down gets some sympathetic stress response. Do your three breaths again to get beyond. Now you know these trigger events are associated with stress, so now you know when to get Para by doing the three breaths.

Be your Inner Dog

Your sympathetic nervous system is an ancient system that allowed our ancestors to react quickly when attacked by pre-historic man-eaters. But you're not being attacked by a tiger are you? You may have to deal with CAVEmen but otherwise you're just looking at your injury reports, going to a meeting with your boss, or making a phone call to find out why someone got hurt. So why do you get that all too familiar stressful emotional response? When you were in your 20s you didn't have this reaction to spreadsheets and phone calls. What happened? I don't mean to insult anyone, but you came to behave like a dog.

Pavlov showed more than a century ago that dogs who naturally salivated when meat powder was put in their mouths (an automatic response) eventually started salivating long before the meat powder entered the picture. They started salivating when the researcher who fed them the meat powder entered the room. Pavlov started using bells and lights in when the meat powder was delivered. Soon enough these dogs started salivating just in response to the bells and lights. They had learned an automatic response. (Have you noticed how your dog starts wagging her tail even before you pet her?)

The same learning can occur with the fear response. The classic study was done by a guy named Watson who took a baby he called "Little Albert" and exposed him to a mouse. Now babies are not afraid of mice (nor were you when you were young) so Albert played with the mouse and pleasantly giggled. Then out of the blue, Watson started banging on a pot to make a loud startling noise behind Albert. This resulted in a startled crying baby. Every time Albert played with the furry mouse he got spooked. After only a couple of these rather mean episodes, Albert would cry and crawl away whenever he saw a mouse. In fact, he'd cry when he saw a rabbit and even a stuffed fuzzy doll. Albert had learned a fear response to an otherwise cute, harmless animal. Does this happen to you too? You bet it does, all the time.

Your ringing phone was a neutral stimulus early on. The only response you had was probably an orienting response and mild curiosity about who is calling. But then one time the phone rang and on the other end was a shift supervisor informing you that one of your team had been injured. Hearing bad news — someone got badly hurt — naturally set off your fear response. All animals react this way when seeing others injured. Humans only have to hear a description of injuries to get this response, especially with people we personally know. When you experience the ringing phone coupled with bad news too many times, a simple ring can cause that adverse reaction regardless who is at the other end.

Who knows, maybe the voice at the other end of the phone is your boss and he is prone to get intense when discussing your job; some may interpret it as anger. An angry person naturally creates a fear response. Pair your angry boss enough times with a phone ring and all it takes is a buzzing cell phone to get that same response.

Patricia… remember Patricia from the previous chapter? Patricia's boss was just another person when you met her. Her shift meetings didn't put Patricia on guard, bored maybe, but nothing special. But the one day Patricia took that stupid broken guard off her loom and she got a surprising angry bark from behind and her boss continued a loud diatribe about how careless and unsafe Patricia was. Patricia's body reacted naturally by tightening up, fouling her stomach, and putting her senses on edge. It took a while to calm down; Patricia felt tense and distressed (the fear response). This reaction became associated with her boss. If her boss followed this interaction with negative labeling and fault-finding most of the times they interacted, Patricia experienced that tense and fearful reaction without even talking to the boss.

There are definite safety ramifications in the way we unconsciously associate our automatic responses to our specific surroundings, people, and processes. Not only to your boss but also to anything around you at the time: your workstation, your coworkers, the office, or a training room. This unconscious response does nothing to improve your safety.

How many other stimuli in your work environment set off the fear response? You may not call it fear, partially because you're used to it (habituated), but it is still uncomfortable — and potentially unsafe. Maybe your learned fear response has been associated with loud, grinding machinery because you've experienced someone getting hurt in the midst of it. Perhaps the vehicle fleet pulling out in the morning has been associated with an explosion. Maybe all you need to see is the door to the plant or the property gate and get tense because you know a CAVEman or grumpy, uptight boss is behind it? If you're always tense around work it is likely that you have a lot of these triggers. They put you at risk. They all relate to something you find threatening because they carry the ghost of threats past.

This is unhealthy and unsafe. Think about what's happening. Your heart is overworked (hypertension), your muscles tighten, and you digestion is turned off. Ever wonder why you get butterflies in your stomach at stressful times? Practice the three breaths that turn off this fear system as many times a day as you need to. You will learn to do it at will and begin to control the fear response. And you'll be safe for it.

You've now learned enough about yourself to consider co-workers who have the same bodily responses (as do supervisors, managers and executives, to be fair). They get the same fear response naturally to threats like falling beams and uptight managers on fault-finding fishing expeditions. How many triggers do your workers experience around the worksite elicit fear when there is not an actual threat? Probably a lot, a whole hell of a lot.

Do you think they are happy to see a frowning manager stalking around?

I was walking around with Tom at a steel smelting plant taking a tour of the fiery cauldron of hell that produces the lava flows that end up as posts for our road signs. I spent the day with an employee team charged with rolling out and managing their behavioral safety program. Tom was their safety manager and champion. I like to take tours of plants so Tom obliged.

On the tour Tom was pointing out hazards he wanted to fix and impartially talking about the most prominent risks at the plant. But what caught my attention was how the folks in different parts of the plant lit up when he walked in with me. Tom had intentionally associated his presence with a pleasant experience every time he interacted with his workers. He smiled, called them by name, asked about their kids or motorcycle, and always praised them for something they were doing to make the plant safer. And for that, when he asked for suggestions or had to discuss some at-risk behaviors, he generally got a lot of interaction, even if it was a hard topic to discuss. He always left with a smile, a thumbs up, and "thanks." As we walked toward his workers they would smile and relax, even when talking about hazards or inspection results.

I see a lot of contrasts in management style on these tours. Darryl (the name has been changed) took me around his electronic parts plant in Arizona. Darryl had a cramped little office full of safety reward swag and looked overwhelmed with all the work he had to do. Certainly he was on his best behavior as he introduced me to his different crews of workers. He knew their names but the interactions were quite formal since I was present, and he left it up to me to ask workers about the hazards they faced and the risks they had to take. I was struck by how workers reacted when he entered their space. I could see heads turning to see who was coming and then quickly turning back to their work. Some supervisors hurriedly stashed paperwork and others who were taking a break quickly returned to their task. When Darryl and I walked up to workers I saw their shoulders arch up to their ears as their bodies tightened. Others grimaced as if a sour stomach cramped up. Most managed a feigned smile when greeting me but there was not much interest in talking. No one wanted to start a conversation.

How did Tom and Darryl elicit these different responses from workers? Over time their behavior while interacting with their workers shaped an automatic response. Imagine when a new worker first meets Tom. Tom is pleasant and asks about the family and hobbies. The new worker experiences an automatic bodily reaction when thinking about her kids. Emotionally she may interpret this as "joy." She talks about her skeet-shooting hobby and her automatic body reaction may be interpreted as "excitement." What Tom does, probably without knowing it, is pair himself with "joy" and "excitement" and he continues to do it every time he enters her workspace and asks similar questions. Over time, just his presence elicits the same positive bodily reaction. These body reactions are further interpreted by other workers and they are genuinely happy to see Tom. Joy, excitement, safety… three words not usually associated with each other.

In contrast, imagine a new hire when she meets Darryl. On her first day she must sit in a quiet room while Darryl gives a safety orientation. He is running a bit late so the first interaction is a formal, rather stiff and uncomfortable welcome to the newbies as he stands in front of them, an officer of their new company. Automatic body reaction? Muscles tense, mind aware, searching for clues. He lectures about the safety rules and consequences for violations. Muscles get more tense as the mind thinks about getting fired. Jaw clinches a bit. When Darryl subsequently does his walk-arounds, fishing, he may approach a fellow worker who has taken off her gloves to get a better feel of the small electronic part she is manipulating. Darryl swoops in abruptly citing the rules and possible consequences. He then slaps a label on the person. Careless. Reckless. This unexpected, unpleasant event makes the new worker jump involuntarily, the tone and content of Darryl's voice sets off the fear response. Her sympathetic nervous system jumps into gear, alerting her body, shutting down digestion, and giving her the interpretation of feeling "nervous." In the

> Being nervous and afraid of a safety pro is a no-win situation.

future Darryl may approach her in the same manner asking about the condition of her lighting and posture. What Darryl did, certainly unknowingly, was pair himself with "nervous" and he continues to make this association whenever in her presence. It doesn't take long for her to experience these body responses just seeing him across the parking lot. She is not the only one making this association. Being nervous and afraid of a safety pro is a no-win situation.

Here we have the fear response in action. And it's not improving the safety of the workplace at all. Over time, there is some habituation to stronger interpretations of fear. The reaction typically lessens to a mere "dread" or "mistrust." Regardless, the body's reaction is not comfortable, healthy or safe. It creates a good CAVEman, a resistor.

Learning to Avoid Safety

What happens next is a principle called conditioned avoidance. This concept goes all the way back to animal research but it most certainly applies to humans; we can get really good at it. Rats were exposed to an aversive stimulus, like a shock, a second after a light turned on. The shock certainly created the fear response. The rats then learned how to make the shock go away by pressing a lever. Eventually, actually quite quickly, the rats learned to push the lever when the light turned on to avoid the shock altogether. Their fear response? They get rid of that too by pushing the lever.

Does Darryl want conditioned avoidance — his workers evading him? Do you? Do you already confront it?

What does avoidance look like on the plant floor? Do folks suddenly disappear when the safety committee or the safety manager come around? Is there no eye contact? Do they go into CAVEman mode when safety comes a calling to keep a comfortable distance? Do workers sit in the back of the meeting room during safety training? Avoidance. It's a major problem in safety work. Workers press the avoidance button at the sight of a safety patrol (or your managers) to avoid being labeled again. And they keep it up because it works!

This avoidance problem gets worse because people generalize to other targets.

Darryl elicits the fear response and workers tighten up and avoid him when he comes around. Darryl becomes a kind of King Midas (who could touch anything and it turns to gold) in reverse. Anything Darryl is associated with also is something to be avoided. Let's see, what might an irritated, impatient safety manager be associated with on their job? Safety meetings? Training? PPE? Forms for inspections or observations?

How do workers "push the lever" to avoid safety? In some cases they start to hide their behaviors. Peers teach one another how to avoid getting caught (I'd do that if I were a fish who could talk.) The safety culture deteriorates. Injuries increase. Pencil whipping is my favorite. One way to avoid dealing with a fear-inducing safety manager is to make sure you always get your reports in on time. And you make sure they don't reveal anything that will have that manager labeling you. So you just fill out the forms saying "Everything's OK" often without even going out and doing the inspection or observation. Pencil whipping.

Avoidance out of fear can be become even more dangerous and unsafe. When faced with aversive stimuli animals start messing up their surroundings and even go and beat up other animals (this is called adjunctive behavior). We are not entirely certain why. Perhaps they are looking for more ways to avoid the aversive stimuli; perhaps it is a reaction to the fear response enacting the fight or flight reaction, who knows? We can't ask a rat to tell us in his own words.

What we do know is that we see this kind of conflict in humans as well. Humans interpret their reaction as "anger" or "frustration." Sometimes you see it, as in the case of the CAVEman, but many times you don't. It is the sort of reactivity that occurs when everyone seems to be saluting and doing what is desired, but behind the scenes they are sabotaging safety efforts or abusing safety resources. I've interviewed a ton of resistant folks. Get them to speak honestly and you'll find they are fighting fear with what is really a misguided bravery. They are typically good folks trying to find an outlet for the arousal that springs from the fear response.

When I tour a plant for the first time, before I chat with anyone, before I look at their injury numbers, before I look at results of safety culture surveys, there is one way I can tell if this learned fear response is present. All I have to do is look around. Is there tobacco stains on the wall? Is the coke machine kicked in? Is there graffiti on the safety board? It tells me almost all I need to know.

People get negatively labeled during fishing expeditions and they act out. Wouldn't you? This is why we must drive fear out of the workplace, as Deming said. Fear is the enemy of safety. Inappropriate labeling is the locus of fear. Choose your labels carefully.

DYSFUNCTIONAL PRACTICE: MANAGING THROUGH FEAR

Fear around hazards keeps us alert and primed for emergency. Fear makes us more aware of our behaviors and in tune with potential severe consequences. Unfortunately, this fear of hazards habituates across time and does not maintain safety behavior.

Managers who manage safety through aversive tactics create fear. This fear gets associated not only with the risks and hazards, but also with the manager and even the safety systems.

Humans avoid fear and therefore, they tend to avoid the manager and safety systems that can get them in trouble. Fear reduces participation in safety programs and increases reactive behaviors that sabotage safety programs.

CHAPTER 6:

Labels Keep Us From Learning

THE DYSFUNCTIONAL PRACTICE OF LABELING PEOPLE can build the fear response with all its repercussions — avoidance, resistance and a deteriorating safety culture. Compounding the dysfunction is the fact that when you label, especially when you label someone "stupid," well, you're probably wrong.

The fact is nobody's stupid. It's simply insulting to take the marvel of the human brain and reduce it to this pejorative label (are you stupid because you don't know the word "pejorative?" Am I smart because it used it in a sentence? See how silly it is).

Intelligence is typically measured as the Intelligence Quotient (IQ) and the fact is that 97.5 percent of us qualify as "intelligent" (68 percent of us qualify as average intelligence). But there are other types of intelligence. Much has been made recently of leadership E.Q. (emotional intelligence). Also consider the special aptitudes mechanics have, the understanding of the natural environment geologists possess and the knowledge of numbers demonstrated by accountants. The pro basketball players of the world show us a kinesthetic (body) intelligence and our favorite artists demonstrate an aesthetic intelligence.

I teach classes of more than 200 students. When I teach them theories around intelligence I lecture how the one type of intelligence, the "g" factor (IQ), soon became three specific types of intelligence, then eight, and then I report that modern intelligence theorists say there may be something like 135 different types of intelligence. I conclude with an affirmation, *"There must be over 200 different types of intelligence because each of YOU brings something special to the world."* Likewise, everyone at your facility, from the engineers, office dwellers, maintenance staff, machinists, workers, and your leaders, has something special to bring to the safety table.

Are we leveraging this fact? Are we connecting with everyone in our company to make our safety program better, more effective at motivating safe behaviors and reducing injuries? Or are we labeling... based on limited information... using our stereotypes? If we are labeling, fishing, or otherwise causing the fear response, we're not learning from our incident investigations (a micro level failure), and we are failing to learn from the collective intelligence of our people on a meta-scale (a macro level failure).

When you assign a negative label like "stupid" or "lazy" you won't be able to tap into the wisdom of your workforce because they will be less likely to talk to you. A derogatory label minimizes the need to collect more information because we think we have arrived at the root cause of a safety issue. We tend not to do the harder work of confirming our perception of the person. In fact, psychology tells us when we label we tend to only look for information that confirms our bias. You ignore the time when the new maintenance guy came around collecting donations for the girls' soccer program but remember vividly the time when he complained that there were no six-foot ladders around the plant except in the loading dock. You use only the information that confirms your stereotype of maintenance folks and your label for the new guy.

It's not a surprise that you're unlikely to approach the cranky maintenance guy to strike up a conversation about tool safety and learn about the ladder problem because you expect the guy to act a certain way.

And, frankly, you are probably tired in general of people complaining so you don't talk to them… failing to learn from the collective intelligence of our people.

Not only does labeling make you less likely to talk and listen to your people, it makes them less likely to talk or listen to you. This two-way inhibition is a disaster for a safety program.

Labeling kills the conversation. Try it and find out for yourself. Go into your workplace and strike up a conversation around safety. In the middle of the conversation, point out a fault and call the crew stupid. See what happens. The conversation stops. You upset people and they clam up. Even if a person agrees with your label there is nothing else to talk about… they just have to try harder not to be stupid. Problem solved? Not.

When folks get labeled, especially the negative labels, not only are conversations stifled, but folks take steps to avoid conversations altogether. Think about our manager Darryl who tends to issue labels when things are not going well and people are frustrated. What do the workers do when Darryl comes around? They try to avoid him. He has punished the interaction. Do you think that his employees are going to come up to him and offer some needed suggestions of how to improve safety on the floor? No way. They may even have a secret whistle that goes out whenever he starts to walk the floor and everyone seems to disappear or get real involved in their task, not looking up. Um…Do YOU hear a faint whistle when you walk out on your plant's floor?

Talk the Talk

I'm a psychologist so I'm used to being around terms like "culture" that have been constructed to describe things that are not tangible. We call terms like this "constructs" because we had to construct a term from scratch to describe something we can't see. "Culture" has been over-studied in industrial/organizational psychology where we argue over silly differences between "culture" and "climate."

Even though I've been trained to deal with such constructs, I had a big problem getting my arms around what a "culture" is. To me the term "safety culture" is an undefined mess of other constructions that don't mean anything either like "value," "beliefs," or "assumptions." Unfortunately, this confusion leads to haphazard attempts at changing safety cultures, often at the expense of confusion. Thus, the term will begin to diffuse into meaninglessness like so many good-ideas-turned-fad before. This is too bad because the real concept of safety culture is profound and can lead to significant improvements.

Fortunately, I'm not your run-of-the-mill psychologist. As a behavioral psychologist I prefer to see parsimony as the goal. Thus, I apply Occam's Razor to terms like "safety culture" to end up with an extensively more useful concept. The definition of Occam's Razor according to Merriam-Webster Dictionary is: "*Entities should not be multiplied unnecessarily. The simplest of competing theories be preferred to the more complex. Explanations of unknown phenomena be sought first in terms of known quantities.*"

Let's try this new definition of safety culture on for size: safety culture is *people talking to each other* and *how that talking impacts safety behaviors.*

Consider a worker telling another about a short cut to a task that involves risk. Consider a supervisor who emphasizes speed in getting a piece of equipment back on line. Consider a leader who tells subordinates to push the equipment upgrades off for yet another year to save costs. In all these instances the safety culture promotes risk through talking — a negative safety culture.

Alternatively, when a worker takes a moment to alert another employee when they are taking a risk, when a supervisor asks his work team about the potential hazards in a job and discusses the safe behaviors that mitigate the hazards, or when a leader asks his subordinates about the safety implications of budget decisions, the safety culture promotes safety through talking — a positive safety culture.

People talking to people about safety occurs through all levels of the organization and is not necessarily top-down or bottom-up.

Note also that safety management systems are just formalized methods of communication:

• Minor Injury/Close Call reporting = talking about incidents that happened instead of hiding them;

• Safety Procedures = written talking about safe behaviors on a job;

• Training = talking, a lot;

The question here is: how effectively are these safety management systems at influencing the critical talking that needs to go on between and among your employees and managers?

The way we're going to solve any problems with our safety management system is to gain insight into the risks people take, and the only way we are going to get insight into the risks people take is by talking to each other. When labels kill the conversation, risks are taken and the system that promotes this risk-taking remains hidden, deep in the culture of silence.

Talking to each other about safety = Safety Culture.

Get people talking..

Icy Triangles

In Heinrich's 1931 seminal book *Industrial Accident Prevention* he offered a powerful metaphor. We will use it to make the next couple of points. His metaphor, the safety pyramid, suggests that for every fatality and serious injury there are a number of minor injuries that could have pointed us to the potential for the more serious incident. Indeed, there are even more near misses (close calls) where an incident occurred but no one got hurt that could point to an eventual serious incident. At the base of the pyramid are the most numerous, minor incidents, behaviors that put people at-risk. Getting visibility into the numerous risks people take will help us to reduce injuries.

Unfortunately, the pyramid got us spending way too much time arguing about ratios of minor injuries to serious ones. Even Heinrich suggested that these ratios vary across industries, time, and other variables. Indeed, data suggest it's logically flawed to blend incidents that are unrelated. Instead, what Heinrich was expounding, especially in the second edition of his book (1941), was that fixing the causes of minor incidents will help prevent more serious incidents. In other words we must learn from the lower levels how to form causal connections.

In my pompous scholarly work I've discussed the human behavior relationship to serious injuries, and evidence showing that at-risk behavior is a symptom of trouble within the system. Further, I've written about how humans typically are not the cause of serious injuries but they can set off latent conditions, left behind by others or flaws in a process, tools, or equipment that lead to energy release (such as in the Deepwater Horizon where inadequate downward pressure and faulty blowout preventers caused an explosion on the deepest oil rig of its time).

I've also written about how complacency, or what scientists call "drift" in human behavior can lead to a normalization of deviance that have led to industrial disasters (if you need a good nap contact me and I'll send you these academic articles).

The human and organizational performance (HOP) folks like Weick and Sutcliffe, who seem to really like their acronyms, write in *Managing the Unexpected* that companies with a pre-occupation for reporting possess characteristics of a high-reliability organization (HRO). These companies seek information from risk identification, hazard identification, precursor events, process deviations, and the like. Discovering causal connections between system factors, behavioral factors and injuries, both common and serious, have everything to do with communication. People talking to each other = "culture."

Heinrich's ratios have lost their punch, but we still see the pyramid as a cautionary tale. The more you can learn from the bottom of the pyramid, the more you can prevent the serious stuff at the top.

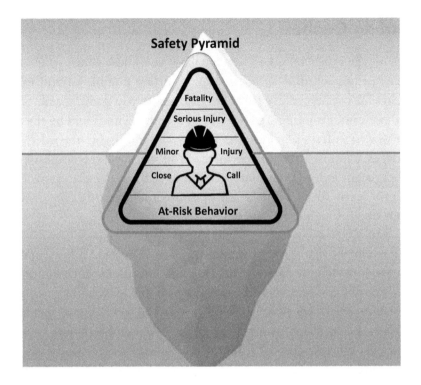

You will often see an iceberg superimposed on the safety pyramid. I was up in Newfoundland doing some training and had a chance to go out and view the icebergs coming down the Labrador current from the Arctic. I mentioned to the safety pro who accompanied me that the icebergs were huge! And he said "That's only the tip of the iceberg. Underwater, that is where most of the iceberg is."

The tip of the iceberg is all you see. In safety, the tip of the iceberg is what is visible to managers. Serious injuries are obvious, they cannot be hidden. If your company has a fatality would everyone in the company know about it? Would the local press know about it? Would the government know about it? Absolutely. Same question: If your company had a serious injury, something that will affect the individual the rest of their life, would we all be aware of the incident? Yes.

I got an Ouchee

Let's hit the waterline now. How much do you know about your workforce's minor injuries? What is your reporting culture around minor injuries? What percentage of minor injuries do you know about? Some of these minor injuries are above the waterline. This could be the case if a worker suffers a cut and seeks first aid and it gets recorded or a manager witnesses the minor injury. You can also see some of the iceberg right below the waterline, although it may be distorted. Here we may learn about a minor injury sometime after the fact or learn about one through the grapevine.

Unfortunately, many minor injuries are not reported. Why? Let's say you are loosening a flange with a wrench and the wrench slips. You bang your elbow pretty good causing a nice bruise. Whatta you gonna do? Go to your supervisor and say *"I got an ouchee"*? These are rough jobs worked by tough people who might find it embarrassing to make a big deal out of something minor. Maybe these types of bangs and bumps are just considered part of the job and not something to report. Bottom line, you're worried that if you tell people that you slipped and banged up your arm on the job you'll earn the label "stupid" or clumsy.

It's possible that you used a cheater bar to get more leverage from your wrench on the flange bolt. The rules are pretty clear against cheater bars but the tool crib is way over at the loading dock and you and your buddies hid some metal tubing just for this purpose. So you bent the rules (and probably the tubing) when you got your bruise. You gonna tell your boss about this? Probably not.

There are other reasons why you may not report a minor injury. What happened the last time you reported an injury? What was your experience? If you had to be taken off the job and go to the principal's office to fill out a long form I bet you wouldn't find it rewarding. You didn't take this job to be a writer and this form asks a lot of questions that take a lot of words... some of which you'd rather not write because it's embarrassing. Then when you're all done you have to assign the incident to a root cause and the top choice on the list to choose from is... "stupid."

We have to acknowledge that sometimes a minor injury may be reported but not recorded. Perhaps because it might embarrass the person you report to (who didn't get the new tool you had requested). And recording a minor injury could hurt their numbers. Minor injuries, or first aids, are typically tracked for the trending that can lead to proactive actions to avert a larger incident. But showing an increase in first aids in your unit can lead to unwanted scrutiny by the safety police or upper management. So best to keep those numbers down.

This fact hit home when I visited a refinery where I was kindly given a tour. The refinery had an excellent safety program overall. My guide was doing a good job looking out for our safety. Beyond the usual orientation and PPE, he frequently alerted us to hazards as we walked through the plant; many times we were walking single file so it was incumbent on the rest of us to point to the hazard as well to deliver the information down the line. He pointed to one protruding plate of metal about head level. I remember pointing it out as well. Perhaps I touched the metal itself, perhaps it had some chemical residue, perhaps my safety gloves were clipped to my belt, perhaps later in the day I scratched my ear? Who knows? But after I got back to the hotel I found some type of chemical burn behind the lobe of my ear and down my neck. I debated for a day whether to report it to the refinery or not.

I hesitated to report this minor burn because I was the safety expert coming to the plant to do an assessment and offer suggestions. It would be embarrassing for me. So it took a couple days to send an email to the safety pro at the plant reporting my small burn and letting him know that it had cleared up. I was willing to complete any minor injury form they required. The email back was surprising. He suggested that I potentially got the rash from another source before arriving at the refinery and there would be no need to report a minor injury. No form. No record. Below the water line.

But don't we want our employees, work team leaders, contractors, and, um, guests to report when they suffer a minor injury? It's true that most incidents don't need to be reported to regulators, but it's also true that reporting can protect both the employee and company's interests if the injury turns out to be worse than expected.

The main reason to encourage our workforces to track minor injuries is to be able to collect the data and learn from it. We can study the data and even use the emerging field of analytics to determine trends that suggest the potential for more severe injuries. Uncovering trends allows us to proactively fix hazards and reduce risk-taking before the more severe injuries raise their ugly head.

We can even learn from the individual minor injury by learning about the situation the worker was in and the behaviors that put the worker at-risk. From this context we can analyze the behaviors to come up with actionable solutions.

Near Misses are actually a Near Hit

Near misses are even deeper underwater. You can dive into the frigid water and kind of see them. My friend and colleague Scott Geller is fond of questioning the use of the words "near miss." He's right; think about it. What actually happens when you nearly miss? You don't miss, you almost missed, but you nearly got HIT. So the words don't apply to incidents when you're walking and slip but catch yourself without actually falling and hitting the floor. Scott prefers the term "Close call." I do too.

Close calls lie deeper underwater because no one gets hurt. There is no harm, no evidence. No harm, no foul, no record. Close calls are typically not reported for the same reasons that minor injuries are skipped over: a) they are embarrassing. Think about when you last tripped and righted yourself in a clumsy body contortion. Of course, the first thing is to look back and discover what you tripped on. What's the second thing you do? You look around to make sure no one witnessed your lack of cool. You don't report these events because it's embarrassing. I typically don't report to my wife my personal clumsy acts. Other reasons that close calls are not reported are because b) close calls happen frequently and seem to be part of the job; c) taking time to report, to be interviewed, and fill out the forms is punishing; and d) close calls can get you in trouble if you are doing something wrong. We've heard all these reasons for not reporting minor injuries … but with close calls there is no evidence, no scratch, bruise, cut, or sprain to cover up.

It's critical to learn from close calls. There are so many more of them… so much to learn from them. We can trend close call data and be proactive about actions to fix hazards and reduce risk-taking in the face of those hazards. But something more personal is going on. Something that gets to the heart of a safety culture (talking to each other about safety = safety culture). Talking about your close calls is a way to help your fellow workers in a very real way.

To get personal I'll tell you another story. I call it "Bless Her Heart."

I was having a great conversation with a new steering team charged with launching a behavioral safety program at a plant that made feminine hygiene products in the southern United States. I was making grand statements like, *"One key to an ideal safety culture that drastically reduces injuries is for everyone to take responsibility for safety,"* and all the southern ladies in the room nodded vigorously. They drank the Kool Aid. They volunteered to be on the team to help build this safety culture and help their fellow workers (mostly women).

I have a trick I like to play on groups like this and I had this set of ladies right where I wanted them. I first get them all to agree to the statement *"Everyone has to be responsible for their own safety and the safety of others."* Everyone always agrees, sometimes enthusiastically. Then I pretend to change the subject and ask, *"What was the last injury you had here at the plant?"* I found out that a high school intern was carrying a stack of papers down some stairs in the front office area. She slipped, fell down the stairs, and broke her ankle. The safety pro on the team told us the details. All the ladies were in a stir. One exclaimed, *"Well bless her heart — is that Doris' daughter who worked here over the summer? That young lady played volleyball and she probably had to miss her high school season."* What a wonderful and caring group of women; they even began planning a bake sale for her.

But then I drop the other shoe in my trick. I interrupted and pointed at the heart-blesser and asked sternly, *"Why did you let that happen?"*

One could hear the collect breath intake as the indignation grew. *"She was an intern… didn't even work for us."* *"She was probably carrying too much and didn't hold the hand rail."* *"She didn't even work in my department. We work out in the plant where there are real dangers like molten plastics and sharp tools. She was up in the front office helping the secretaries."*

I continued with the punch line. *"Now hold on ladies… I just said that everyone has to take responsibility for safety… you all nodded!"* I then said, mocking confusion, *"So therefore you take responsibility for her fall and broken ankle. So…. (pause for effect) why did you let it happen?"*

They continued complaining as they justified how this situation was different and her fall was not their responsibility. They were not happy campers at this point. I thought I had made a critical mistake and lost their trust. I was about to apologize. But then something subtle yet culturally significant happened. A couple of women started asking the right questions: *"Where did this happen?"* *"What else was going on?"* *"Had she been given training?"*

Finally, it was the bake-sale planner who asked, *"She fell down stairs right? Were those stairs by the entrance door out front? You know, the ones near the outside courtyard where some of us go on smoke breaks? Yeah, yeah… those stairs get kind of wet when we all walk back in after a dewy morning."*

It was that point that the heart-blesser, quietly, yet clearly, said *"Gals, you know, I've slipped on those very stairs when they've been wet."* Many of the women nodded. *"When I slipped and caught myself I thought, 'I wish someone would take care of this'."* More nods. Some around the room made pre-dictable statements like *"They should do something; they need to put down some of that non-slip tape on those stairs."*

But then the heart-blesser uttered a statement worth a thousand bake sales: *"I guess when I had slipped before … I was embarrassed … so I never told anyone."* The group got quiet. Then more quiet when heart-blesser said, as if to herself, *"And if I would have said something ... something could have been done about it... that poor young girl would have played volleyball last season."*

Lesson delivered: By not taking personal responsibility to report the near miss, the stair hazard was not fixed and this led to an injury. Everyone who experienced those wet stairs was responsible. Taking personal responsibility for the safety of others does not only mean coaching each other when we see a need to reduce risk-taking. It also means we report our own behavior and our own incidents, even if they are close calls and embarrassing. Because when we do we might help someone down the line, someone we don't even know.

This unfortunate story can be played out almost anywhere — with sobering lessons. My friend Steve Roberts from Safety Performance Solutions tell the more tragic story of being called to a cement manufacturing plant down in Texas. The plant had suffered a fatality. Steve was, among other things, helping with the investigation. A man was carrying about 40 pounds of compound over his shoulder on a skyway positioned above the huge vats of mixing product. There were grates in the walkway that could be removed so different compounds could be poured directly in the vat. As he walked, he stepped on a grate that buckled and collapsed. He fell into the machinery below, suffocating in the cement vat.

Steve recalls a supervisor saying at one point during the investigation meeting, *"We all walked over that grate... it would clatter around because it had warped over time as we carried heavy loads over it. I just started walking around it instead of on it because it scared me."*

He ultimately arrived at a sobering conclusion: *"I should have reported that and got it fixed. Heck, any of us could have... And poor Joe would still..."*

Back to the feminine hygiene plant. Why did this injury to the young woman happen? To be sure, it's simple to conclude that *"the young woman did not use the handrail"* and chalk it up to human error... she was careless, stupid. But what is the solution to human errors? Typically it would be more exhortations for everyone to "Use Hand Rails" by way of signs and meetings. This may change behavior — but only for a week before drifting back to old habits. And the incidents reoccur.

The next likely conclusion, also easy to arrive at, is, "*They* (management) *did not maintain the equipment and facilities adequately to reduce the hazard of the stairs.*" The typical "Us vs. Them" drama ensues with workers blaming management for the problem and management pointing at workers as the source of the problem.

I hope the irony of this situation is not lost on anyone when you think back to your first grade teacher saying, "*When you point at someone else (with your index finger), you have three fingers pointing back at yourself.*"

Indeed, the missing factor key to these scenarios was a safety culture where everyone takes responsibility for the safety of others. You take responsibility for the safety of others through reporting near misses and minor injuries, identifying hazards formally, and coaching peers when anyone sees behaviors that put workers at risk. You take responsibility for the safety of others when you give safety talks at tailgate meetings, join safety committees, and praise each other for safe practices. You take responsibility for the safety of others when you actively participate in the safety culture.

It is quite probable that you, personally, never slipped on those stairs or stepped around that grate. But it is quite probable that you, personally, have had an incident that happened in your area where you were too embarrassed, scared, or thought to little of it to report. And, because you didn't report it or just complained about management to a coworker, you did not do your part to build a culture of freely reporting your incidents so others can learn and act on them.

But if you set the right example and others see your courage, they may also see how speaking up can make a safer workplace. Then they will muster the courage to do the same. Our safety management systems must be built correctly to support a culture of reporting. This means no attribution or punishment, no long embarrassing forms, and, most importantly, you have a process where close calls get publically acted on by addressing hazards. Excellent safety management systems reinforce people for reporting. This does not mean giving out a prize or pat on the back. Reporters get reinforced for reporting because things got better because they reported. *"I reported a problem and it got fixed. Everyone will know I did my part to build our safety culture into one where reporting is what we do, what we value, and what we exp*ect." Bake sales are not enough.

Behavior — the Bottom of the Iceberg but the most valuable

What's at the bottom of that iceberg? Behaviors.

Behaviors are actions — physical and verbal actions that others can experience when they are around you. That makes behaviors particularly open to observation by self or others. Behaviors produce outcomes. Behaviors such as putting on personal protective equipment, using three points-of-contact on a six- foot ladder, or double-checking your wiring will help someone stay safe in the midst of hazards. Conversely, behaviors such as pulling your respirator to the side of your face during a hot day may put you at-risk of injury in the face of certain hazards like paint fumes.

Behaviors form the base of the iceberg because they are so personal. Behaviors generate your successes, true. They are the locus of your greatness, kindness, and usefulness. Behaviors also produce your errors. They can indeed be the source of embarrassment, hard feelings, and reprimand. Behaviors are plentiful. Behaviors happen all the time, continuously, often without consideration. We may not even think about how important they are. Yet behaviors are critical, crucial, vital, central, essential, fundamental, and any other word my Thesaurus can come up with, to safe operations in your workplace.

Your behaviors help you stay safe or put you at-risk. Consistent engagement in safe behaviors reduces the number of close calls and minor injuries. And, most importantly, safe behaviors should decrease the probability of serious injury and fatalities. If your employees engage in behaviors that put them at-risk, those additional risks will result in more close calls and injuries and increase the probability of something more serious.

Let's understand that most of the risks we take are unintentional; we are unaware that our behavior is putting us at risk. Certainly, new workers, Green Hats, perform many behaviors that unintentionally put them at-risk. They just don't have the experience to know the plethora of risks around the worksite and how to avoid them. They are far more likely to be at-risk than more experienced workers who have experienced close calls or seen injuries because of these dangers.

Personally, I am very aware of how *unaware* of hazards I am when I visit your worksite. I know what I don't know. I am certain that my behavior can put me unconsciously at-risk. When I tour a worksite, I lock my hands behind my back and walk exactly two steps behind my guide. When she stops, I stop. When she turns, I turn. When she points to a hazard, so do I. I am unaware of the hazards so I don't know which of my behaviors might put me at-risk. It could be one wrong step into the line of fire of a forklift and splat. So I rely on the experienced guide and don't stray.

But even the most experienced workers I've talked to admit that they find themselves engaged in unintentional risks. This is because the workplace is constantly changing. Processes get revised, equipment get upgraded, leaders turnover, and there is always a new group of unintentionally at-risk millennial workers rustling about. If veteran workers get complacent about their safety behaviors they may find that what kept them safe in the past may indeed put them at-risk in the future.

Everyone is unintentionally at-risk in a fluid workplace environment. But one person's newfound awareness of a risk could be another person's path to safety. It's critical to periodically have a second set of eyes on a task to consider the unintentional risks caused by the worker's behavior, and then have a conversation to pass on a new awareness (talking to about safety each other = safety culture). Information-sharing can transform unintentional at-risk behaviors into behaviors that keep people safe in the face of danger. I'm talking not only about the person who was observed, but also others performing that same task as well. If we do not encourage workers to observe each other and discuss their findings, we allow unintentional at-risk behaviors to remain submerged and hidden.

Let's admit it — some of the risks we take are intentional. We choose the stepladder instead of retrieving the correct ladder for the job; we skip the pressure check and go straight to decoupling hoses; we jump down in that confined space without a permit to retrieve a dropped tool. When we find ourselves in a position to take a risk, we weigh the potential outcomes and usually choose the path of least resistance... like the water following the grade with the most slope. We choose the stepladder because it's more available, skip the pressure check because it takes too much time, and we jump down into the confined space to save the trouble of admitting our mistake to the boss when we ask for a permit.

> One person's newfound awareness of a risk could be another person's
> path to safety..

Let me state the obvious: a key ingredient to reducing intentional at-risk behavior is to know it is happening. Only then can we analyze the reason why the person found themselves in the position to take the risk and considered it a good idea. If we find out <u>why</u> they did it then we can do something about it. Unless we call them stupid.

Unfortunately, we typically stop any real analysis when we label and blame the person. In many cases, the intentional at-risk behavior violates some training or rule. This can begin a discipline process. Discipline systems can be highly effective at reducing risk-taking and subsequent injuries when used properly and consistently. The threat of discipline can shape worker behavior away from intentional risks when well executed.

But consider discipline the "nuclear option." It can be highly effective but also highly destructive to a safety culture. This is because discipline tools often shape supervisor and leader behavior to the point they default to reprimanding as the primary tool to reduce at-risk behavior. They go fishing for trouble, engaging in fault-finding.

I recall a story of a man in South Africa who was caught without his safety gloves by a supervisor who immediately fired him. This supervisor had left his construction trailer to go discuss some blueprint instructions with an engineer and decided to walk through his site to check the quality of work and fish for safety rule violations. The man who was "caught" was working in a ditch at this construction site and had his safety gloves lying on the dirt. The supervisor immediately called him out of the ditch, berated him, and sent him offsite without a job. The incident of a behavioral violation of the rules was reported to the safety manager.

The safety manager refused to accept the firing because the man had three young children at home and needed the job. Such a small infraction shouldn't impact those young lives. The following day the safety manager called the laborer into her office with the supervisor to learn what had happened. After interviewing the man she discovered that he had been working for about an hour in the sun and heat. He began to find it difficult to see through his safety glasses because they had filmed up with sweat and dirt. So he removed his gloves temporarily to clean his safety glasses for better visibility, something he does from time to time. He would put on the PPE before starting work again. During the walk-around the supervisor saw him right at the moment when he replaced his glasses but before he bent over to put the gloves back on. The man was weeping. He had received the nuclear option for a relatively minor infraction. Hearing the full story, the supervisor agreed to put him back on the job.

These interactions and threats of reprimand and discipline make employees hide their behaviors that put them at-risk. Why would anyone hide behaviors that could result in injury? You'd think we would want to know when we are at-risk. I guess the first point is that most of the time we are unintentionally at-risk. We are not even aware of the risk being taken. The young man in South Africa could have very well have left his gloves on the ground after cleaning his glasses and proceeded to work unaware of his risk, at least for some time. If this happens to him (and you) it is probably happening throughout the workforce sweating in the hot sun. It would be useful to know how often this happens so we can analyze the situation and figure out a solution.

But what if we are consciously engaging in an intentional risk, choosing the step ladder or skipping the pressure check? We do it because the risk/reward calculation adds up, but do we want our managers to know about it? No. We tend to look around before taking the intentional risk to assure it's hidden. Sometimes fellow employees and managers are even complicit in the risk-taking. The calculation helps keep the numbers down, the fracking assembly gets broken down hours quicker and this pleases the client. Intentional risks are not something we talk about unless we are planning with others how to get away with them. This is how we came up with the secret whistle that alerts us to management's presence.

At-risk behaviors remain hidden for a multitude of reasons. This is highly unfortunate of course. When we have visibility into behaviors that put us at-risk we possess a powerful tool to reduce injuries. We better understand why these behaviors are occurring. And what we understand we can manage. Our science knows how to change behavior, intentionally and positively, in a way that sustainable. More on that in the upcoming chapters.

Our at-risk behaviors are submerged way underwater, given no light, no visibility, placed at a distance where it is very hard to see them. Just like the bottom of the iceberg. We've got to find a way to shine a light at the bottom of this iceberg, to make the bottom of the iceberg visible. Who else resides at the bottom of the iceberg with you? Your peers, the folks you work with. They're in the best position to identify risks. To know the situation that put a peer in the position to take the risk. They know why the risk was taken. They are best positioned to interact and discuss the risk (talking about safety to each other = safety culture). They can change the behaviors associated with the risk. And, they all have the most to gain from reducing risk. I tell you, peers make all the difference. They are like scuba divers exploring the bottom of the iceberg.

One substantial advantage we have when scuba diving around the bottom of the iceberg is that, by their very nature, behaviors are observable. You know when you perform a behavior and others can see you do it (if they are around). You can count your behaviors. You see the behaviors in context and you correlate them to other things happening that are related to the behavior.

We designed behavioral safety (aka behavior-based safety) for this purpose. Peer-to-peer observation and feedback allows us to scrutinize the bottom of the iceberg. Peers are in the best position to observe behavior and have culture-defining conversations to make behavior safer. Peers are also in the best position to record behaviors confidentially and pass it on to their team so they can identify areas of risk. We can trend risk, analyze it, and make the changes to the environment, to the system, that lead to sustainable changes in behavior.

Having the commitment to get to the bottom of the iceberg, identify at-risk behavior and do something about it is dependent on your safety culture. I argue to anyone who will listen that safety culture is not some value-laden, touchy-feely, fuzzy construct of an imaginary utopia. Instead, <u>safety culture is people talking about safety and listening to each other</u>. Simple, huh? You can see conversations, engage in conversation, and experience their consequences. Managers can talk and listen, workers can talk and listen… its universal and it makes an impact.

To be sure, conversations can also hurt your safety program. Workers and managers can discuss how to hide at-risk behavior. Workers and managers can complain about the management systems designed to help them stay safe. They can run through safety meetings in monotone voices, teach each other how to pencil whip forms, and outright lie about inspections or preventative maintenance. More insidious is our labeling, a type of talk that makes it far less likely anyone will report at-risk behavior. We all label. We all look at at-risk behavior and go,

"Stupid. Stupid. Stupid." Call someone stupid and see if they continue talking.

We can and must speak up about at-risk behavior. Can the conversations happening all the time among workers (and with managers) influence safe behavior? Can they point out risk, have a discussion about it, and come up with alternative safe behaviors? You bet. Take it further — can those same conversations support other aspects of your safety program? Can they identify hazards, come up with better processes, and share best practices? A positive safety culture is one where people talk about safety — a lot. A positive safety culture identifies at-risk behavior and talks honestly about it, turning the iceberg upside down and making the bottom visible.

DYSFUNCTIONAL PRACTICE:
KILLING THE CONVERSATION

Not only does labeling make you less likely to talk and listen to your people, it makes them less likely to talk or listen to you. This two-way inhibition is a disaster for a safety program.

Safety culture is not some value-laden, touchy-feely, fuzzy construct of an imaginary utopia. Instead, <u>safety culture is people talking about safety and listening to each other</u>. You can see talking, engage in talking, and experience the consequences of talking. Managers can also talk and listen, workers can talk and listen... its universal and it makes an impact.

A key ingredient to reducing at-risk behavior is to know it is happening. Only then can we analyze the reason why the person was in in the position to take the risk. Only workers truly know the at-risk behaviors occurring; we need them to talk to us. Otherwise, risks will be hidden.

The premier safety culture is when your peers coach peers (talking) when anyone sees behaviors that put workers at risk, and when peers praise each other for safe practices.

PART 2:
FUNCTIONAL PRACTICES

CHAPTER 7:

Label the Behavior, Not the Person

BEHAVIOR IS NEUTRAL. With this perspective we can create real solutions by analyzing why a worker was put in a position to take a risk. We want our approach to behaviors to be as open to unbiased analysis as the elements of physics and chemistry. Importantly, as we've discussed throughout this book, this frees us from labeling and gives us the opportunity to assess the true cause of at-risk behavior.

At this point I hope I've got your attention of the dysfunctional practices that destroy a safety culture. Our all-too-human tendencies to label people when things go wrong lead us to blame workers instead of finding the true cause of behaviors that put workers at risk. These human tendencies are nothing more than illusions that lead to fishing expeditions by managers and supervisors that create a fear response in workers. Labeling and fishing expeditions lead to avoidance and lack of talking about safety; not only workers avoiding managers but workers resisting management systems put into place to keep them safe. When we label people as "stupid" or "lazy" or "careless" we throw up barriers to the very behaviors we desperately want our workers to engage in.

You Need Rehab

How do we shatter this illusion? How do we get past the catharsis-seeking, socially reinforced, attribution errors our brains use as short cuts to explain the actions of others? In a sense we are socially addicted to labeling and need rehab. I'm talking about focused rehab where we intentionally practice a new way of approaching at-risk behaviors. The first step in our rehab is to understand what behavior is, what it does, and how it is controlled.

There is an old adage in behavioral science: behavior is governed by discernible laws and our job is to uncover the reasons why people do what they do. B.F. Skinner, our behaviorist guru, summed it up nicely by saying, *"You can only understand behavior by controlling it."* That is what we ultimately want. We want to **CONTROL** the behaviors that put people at risk, either directly through their actions or indirectly when their actions impact others (are you reading this leaders)? Control mechanisms can certainly be used for evil, to win friends and influence your kids. But our aim is to change behavior to reduce injury. Let's consider the process of behavior change.

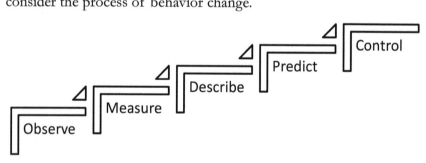

To change behavior in this positive way we must be able to apply the principles of behavior science. I've dedicated my career to devising applications that predictably control behavior in the workplace. We don't want to just throw random interventions into the workplace to see what sticks. In fact, this flavor-of-the-month approach to changing behavior is yet another dysfunctional practice. We must be able to predict the outcomes of our interventions before we attempt to intervene.

If you can **PREDICT** behavior you can control it. That's a good, solid connection. But these are only the *final* steps to manage behavior. To predict anything we must first understand it. Weather prediction is based on a clear understanding of how air pressure, temperature, and geography combine. Likewise, we should understand how our personal learning history, the immediate environment around us, and greater organizational systems combine to impact behavior. Understanding these factors is the basis of our predictions.

I tell my students often, *"The only reason I understand this stuff so well is that I spend a lot of my time describing it to you."* When you describe something, putting it in your own words, your brain processes the information on a much deeper level, considering the information in different contexts and consequences. You understand it better.

Similarly, to understand behavior sufficiently we must first and foremost **DESCRIBE** the behaviors we observe. Our description should not be based on our biases and limited perception. The ancients described their world and afterworld to their satisfaction with myth and mystery. We don't want to manage safety with myth and mystery — although plenty of consultants will sell you some if you buy into their brand of magic elixir. Applying haphazard programs based on some mythical understanding of how to control behavior is not sustainable. Indeed, such non-scientific programs may also be counter-productive to your programs and dangerous for your people.

Instead, behavioral descriptions must be clear, operational, and free of fluff. Descriptions must be similar to what scientists and engineers use when describing the elements of physics and chemistry. Scientists describe the basic elements of our world through the properties of electrons, protons, and neutrons. Therefore, they are able to understand how these basic elements combine into molecules and predict their interaction with other molecules. The result? Society is able to apply all of this understanding to help us control our lives. Even the mighty headache succumbs to the laws of chemistry when confronted by aspirin.

We should follow the example of science and make our behavioral descriptions operational. Operations in your business, in any business, are how things get done. So we need to grasp how the behaviors we are analyzing get things done, how they operate. Making behaviors operational will be part of our description.

Have you heard the old adage: *You can't manage what you can't measure?* Frankly, if you cannot measure something, you're merely guessing. There is too much at stake in safety to guess. Your job, in fact everyone's job, indeed the job of ALL your safety management systems and processes is to **MEASURE** behavior. Because it takes discipline, measurement is the hardest management practice to execute, yet the most essential. However, your rehab requires a discipline that allows you to blast past your ingrained biases and human tendencies to quantify business operations as they really exist.

And that discipline is practiced through observation.

So, before you have your meetings to discuss what to do about your injury rate, before you muse with others why your workers are taking risks, and certainly before you create or change your safety management systems to promote safe behavior — before all of this — go out and observe. Simply watch. See what you discover.

Now don't be creepy in how you go about doing this. I once knew a general manager who wanted to improve the performance of his plant. He suspected inefficiencies so he went out to find them. But instead of wearing his company overalls, probably finely pressed with his rank insignias and medals, he borrowed a contractor's pure white outfit to be a sneaky spy. Yes, an undercover boss. Since he was biased going into this fishing expedition he naturally found what his biases led him to look for through chumming the waters. But when news got around that the boss was seen out and about in disguise, well, let's just add that to the dysfunctional practices list.

Watch, just watch. No hiding. Ask permission first before you watch. No fishing for what you expect to find. Don't seek attributions. Put your biases to bed. You're not looking for someone to do something wrong. You're not looking through the lens of your rule book. Put your own personal experience with the job aside as well; it will only lead you to find faults. This is not a fishing expedition to find faults. It is an exploration to find opportunities to improve safety. Let's go explore!

OBSERVATION is the first functional practice in your rehab. And it is easy. The hard part is putting aside those very human tendencies toward bias, attribution, and fault-finding.

Behavior is easy to observe. The properties of behavior make it particularly open to observation. First, behavior is omnipresent. It is prolific in your life, my life, and the lives of your workers (and managers). Second, behavior is visible, out in the open. You can see it— unlike attitudes, beliefs, values and all the other constructs we've built to supposedly understand behavior. Why seek out covert in-the-head unknowns when behavior is right there in front of us to be observed? Third, we can see the effects of behavior, what it accomplishes. Then we can understand *why* the behavior is happening (in our next chapter). All we need to change and improve is observable.

In our modern world machines can measure for us. My "smart" watch can count how many steps I take in a day. My car can tell me my moment-by-moment gas mileage. Soon, I'm sure my refrigerator will inform me how many calories I'm planning to consume. In industry, bar codes count productivity and analyze consumer patterns. These same bar codes can make sure a grocery selector is at the right skid or if the roustabout actually executed that preventative maintenance word order. Yes, today technology delivers us access to enormous amounts of data on human behavior.

Direct observation is the only real way to understand human behavior.

It is easy to get caught up in cool technology and the cool graphs and statistics available through aggregated data. For now, YOU need to go to the source and observe. Direct observation is the only real way to understand human behavior.

So that's your homework. Go out, ask permission, and observe. Don't worry if the people you observe will be on their "best behavior." You're not looking for right and wrong, because behavior is neutral.

Behavior is Neutral

Get this in your head; tattoo it on the back of your hand to remind you. *Behavior is neutral.* This simple mantra will set your rehab in motion.

Behavior is not right or wrong, good or bad. It just is.

Physics and chemistry consider their basic elements as neutral, not good or bad, right or wrong. They only describe the elements on their basic observable traits and understand them best when they interact in certain controlled situations. Elements themselves are neutral, they just are, but when they interact they have predictable outcomes. It is the *outcomes* that are not neutral. This sober analysis has led to some of the most amazing applications of our modern age. Chemical compounds that save lives, machines that fly, industrial plants that make these medicines and flying machines along with lubricants, propellants, explosives, computers, genetic testing, and the list goes on, exponentially nowadays. Take good note, however, that this is the same physics and chemistry that can kill and maim. Neutral elements… positive or negative outcomes.

I'm going to take a risk to prove this point, one that may hurt my reputation with safety professionals. But I'm going to publish my scandalous confession in this safety book. I am admitting to you right now that the whole time I've been writing this book, the entire time spanning months, I haven't been wearing a hard hat! There, now you know, no hard hat ever touched my head the whole time.

Was I "wrong" to have forsaken a hard hat while writing? Would I have been "right" to do so? No. If I wore a hard hat while writing at my computer, it would not make me safer. It would just make me look ridiculous. This is because behavior is neutral, not right or wrong. Thus, putting on a hard hat is not "right," it is an action that must be defined by the situation you're in.

The situation in which behavior occurs makes all the difference. It is the situation that determines behavior (we'll discover this in the next chapter) and, therefore, it is the situation that *defines* behavior as "safe" or "at-risk."

Can you think of a situation where wearing a hard hat will keep me safe? Certainly, you probably have a lot of situations in your work spaces in which the simple behavior of putting on a hard hat would indeed keep me safe. That situation would define my behavior as "safe," and as an added bonus you could tell me *why* my behavior would keep me safe (a central ingredient to change my behavior).

Consider your plant's rules regarding hard hats. I'll bet you define the situations and places in which hard hats must be worn.

I'll prove my point further. This morning I bent at the waist... all the way to the floor! Was that "wrong"? You can easily think of a situation where bending at the waist will put me at-risk for injury — perhaps if I was picking up a 40-pound load and twisting to put it on a truck bed. In this case it would be the situation that caused my behavior to put me at-risk. The behavior itself, bending at the waist, is neutral. This morning I was not picking up loads. Instead, I was doing yoga (because I'm getting old and my body hurts if I don't). I look pretty awkward so I do it alone using a website teacher. This morning she had me do what is known as a "forward fold," better known as "bending at the waist." I did the behavior this morning. In this situation of my morning stretches, bending at the waist probably made me safer today because it loosened my back.

We could go on and on. Reach out and grab your coffee by the handle. Is that wrong? Is there a situation where you can reach out and stick your fingers in some active equipment where they can get crushed? Same behavior, different situations. It is the situation that defines the behavior as "safe" or "at-risk."

Your processes, your procedures, your equipment and facilities, your policies, your supervision, your programs, your training, your meetings — all of these are the very "situations" we are talking about.

Here is the sobering yet empowering question: who is in control of the situation your workers are put into, the ones that lead to at-risk or safe behaviors? You are.

This point is a critical change of mindset central to your rehab. When you consider a behavior as neutral, *it is the behavior that needs to be labeled, not the behaver.* To label a behavior, we need to understand the situation surrounding the behavior. We must analyze how the situation put the worker in the position to take that risk in the first place. And, in the end, we want to learn to design situations for workers that put them in the position to engage in safe behaviors.

Approach any incident with a clear understanding of the cause and effect relationships between the behaviors related to the risk, and the reasons why that person, either knowingly (on purpose) or unknowingly found themselves in a position to take that risk.

Approach any incident with a clear understanding of the cause and effect relationships between the behaviors related to the risk, and the reasons why that person, either knowingly (on purpose) or unknowingly found themselves in a position to take that risk. (Feel free to read this sentence as much as you need so it sinks in real deep.)

We're talking about applying a different mindset here. Do you notice the distinct way of looking at and understanding behavior? Instead of assigning a label ("stupid," "lazy"), observe behavior as a neutral source of information that can lead you to an analysis providing solutions that change these behaviors for the better.

Labels are Adjectives. Make Safety a Verb

I've assigned your first step in our rehab journey: simply observe behavior. Now you need to get good at describing the behaviors you observed. How you describe behavior makes all the difference because your description is the basis of your analysis and your solutions. These behavioral descriptions should populate your training, your procedures, and your analyses/investigations. Most importantly, labeling the behavior instead of the behaver will break our addiction to blaming/fear and help us arrive at solution-oriented practices through our interactions with workers.

In my experience seeing safety programs around the world in action (or inaction), I've come to realize that *words matter* in your descriptions of behaviors. They not only communicate but can shape the very approach you take to your safety programming. They can bog you down or they can liberate your safety culture.

Consider the term *"Safety."* Safety is a chameleon word. A word used in so many different ways.

"Safety" is most often a NOUN when we decree *"Safety first."* This may seem like a great slogan that would inspire the workforce to think through the safety implications of their actions. However, the slogan may also just be a feel-good sign to hang on the wall with no real benefit. W. Edwards Deming called these "exhortations." Exhortations, Deming told us, create the illusion that exhorted outcomes are achievable and if employees simply tried harder, they would do better. These calls for action can offend the worker — they do not inspire. As time passes the messages become washed out. Without real change workers stop paying attention to cheap exhortations.

"Safety" often is also an ADJECTIVE used to label a particular quality of another word. Consider the sentence: *"You are an unsafe employee."* First of all, how can someone be un-something? A un-person doesn't exist. Second, when you use adjectives you label the subject of your sentence. We may as well say, *"You are stupid."* Your safety programs languish, unleashing apathy, when driven by labels. We've been through this, don't use labels; adjectives are used to label.

"Safety" can be an ADVERB when it modifies verbs by indicating a place, time, or manner, such as, *"I'm going to have to write you up for not climbing that ladder safely."* Here "safely" is supposed to be describing the manner of climbing the ladder. Ironically, it does not indicate how to use the ladder without injury.

In none of these grammatical uses — noun, adjective, adverb — is our word "safety" actually <u>accomplishing</u> anything. For action to occur — and we need action in our description of behavior — we need safety to be a verb. A VERB is a word used to describe an action. *"Safety" is not a verb, but it needs to be.*

It may sound good but *"be safe"* is not a call to action; it's a call for inaction. Yes indeed. The best way to be safe is not to act at all, not to come into contact with hazards, and not work. But that's not reality. In the work world we constantly act. And proper actions are badly needed to create safe outcomes. We need to engage the guards, put on PPE, read instructions, talk to others — we need to act.

Safety requires behaviors to happen.

Behaviors are verbs because behaviors are actions. Safety requires behaviors to happen.

Your description of observed behaviors must contain true action verbs. Action verbs make them operational; when someone operates machinery or a vehicle they are <u>doing</u> something. When Patricia operates her loom she is acting in a way that her behaviors are producing a desirable outcome. She pushes her shuttle downward and in doing so this operation forms the fabric she is working on. Behaviors are actions that *operate* on the environment. That's why in behavioral science we have a scientific name for behaviors: "*operants.*"

To describe behavior, our operant, we need to define what the behavior is operating on and why. After stating the action, we should say what the action is operating on, give some context, and finally state the purpose for this action.

Consider the following sentence structure when instructing someone how to operate:

- **Do What?**   (Action Verb)
- **To What?**   (Subject)
- **When?**   (Context)
- **To Achieve What?**   (Purpose)

For example:

"*Put the key ...*

   in your pocket...

      after you lock out the machine ...

         to remove the risk of energy being turned on by another worker."

This sentence has all necessary the components. It describes a clear operation. It tells you the context in which the operation should occur. And it suggests the consequence of the action. This behavioral description helps the operator discriminate their course of action. When worded correctly, your safety directions can help workers discriminate what behaviors will keep them safe and which put them at risk.

So build a disciplined approach to describing behaviors in a way that create action. Use this sentence structure when you train, write instructions, give prompts, provide feedback and when you record behaviors in incident reports, JSAs, and in BBS analyses.

Wanna give it a try? Go out to where the work is done, ask permission, observe, and describe a behavior that you observed. Use the sentence structure above. Go ahead, do it, I'll wait.

Can your Ancestors Behave?

How did you do with your observation and description homework? Actually, you should have done the observation at work, so it is not technically homework, I guess it is work-work.

Did you notice that behaviors happen quickly? As soon as you notice a behavior it is gone and the worker is on to the next behavior (unless he was taking a nap). You may have felt that you don't have time to write everything down because you may miss something. Don't worry; behaviors happen all the time, constantly. You don't have to capture every one. And since work is often cyclical, you'll have another chance to observe behaviors within the same task when the workflow comes back around.

Did you ask permission, only to worry the workers you observed were on their "best behavior" (note: behavior is neutral, there is no "best") and you didn't observe reality? I bet you still saw behavior that you thought put workers at-risk along with the behaviors that helped keep them safe. Indeed, you may have learned something about safe performance as they demonstrated their versions of safe behaviors.

Was it hard not to look at behaviors in the context of the safety rules? Are workers doing the behaviors because they are following rules or because they are trying to avoid hazards? I'm willing to bet there was not a rule book in sight but the hazards were front and center.

Did you worry that you didn't know their particular job very well and wouldn't know what to look for? All the better. Fresh eyes are more analytical because they are less biased by experience.

Don't fret, your observation skills will get better with practice. Practice every day. Let's keep refining those skills a bit more to make your behavioral descriptions more operational. It's part of your rehab.

Look at what you wrote after your observation. Is the first word or two an action verb or are they being verbs that merely express states of being. *Ralph appeared confused while decoupling the hose.* There is no action in this description. This is simply your interpretation of his mental state. Interpretation = bias; attribution = label. How do you solve Ralph's problem? Do you tell him not to be confused? Retrain him? You're trapped.

Other *being verbs* are actually outcomes of other behaviors. I bet you fell for this one in your homework! *Brenda was not wearing her safety glasses when testing the adhesives.* Not wearing safety glasses is a state of BEING; it is not an action. Wearing PPE is a state of being. Following rules is a state of being, as is "compliance." Folks, Being is not Doing. You need to go back and find out the behaviors that led to this state of Being. What actions caused the Being? What do actions DO to BE... DO... be...Do...be...DO (musical notes here).

Verbs that are not Being are Actions. This is the sweet spot! A key part of your rehab. Actions are actually, factually happening. *Ralph inserted the pressure gauge upside down when decoupling.* Now we have a factual indication of what happened, something we can act on. Remember, if Ralph is acting in this way so are others who find themselves in the same situation.

You can tell you have an action sentence if you can actually visualize it. A good test is if a whole group of observers watch an action and describe it the same way. When you describe Ralph's behavior as *"appeared confused"* I seriously doubt others will have the same description. Ralph's behavior will register differently to different people based on their expectations, biases, attributions, and labels. If all of you are using action verbs, describing specifically what happened, you'll have agreement.

Another way to know you have an action sentence is if you can give the behavioral description to someone and they can perform the action described just as you saw it. If they can act on your description then you're describing an action (duh).

Another way to test for action is the Ancestor Test. Consider this part of your rehab as well. The premise to the test is the fact that all of our ancestors are dead. Which brings us to the test: *If your ancestor can do it, then it is not a behavior... because they are dead.* Dead people cannot behave. They cannot perform actions and operate on their environment, no matter what the situation. If you don't want to take my word for it, go to the nearest grave yard, dig up a casket, open it and demand: *lay still!* Was the dead person able to lay still? Then laying still is not a behavior. Now demand: *Put on your safety glasses!* Can they do it? No! Then putting on your PPE is a behavior because it is active.

My son Forrest used to be quite the challenge to his kindergarten teachers. The boy was hyperactive, especially in social situations. He was smart as a whip answering questions and doing his tasks, but would always be out of his seat and talking with others, disrupting class. We knew about this because we were told at each parent/teacher conference and with numerous notes home complaining about his "behavior."

I recall vividly one note that came home from his gym teacher: *Forrest was dismissed from gym class because he did not sit still.* First of all, sitting still in gym class? Really? Are you not supposed to be active in physical education (gym) classes? Secondly, Forrest's ancestors can *"sit still"* quite nicely can't they? I guarantee they are doing it now.

What instructions was he given in gym class to begin with? *Sit still and shut up.* And we wonder why he didn't change his behavior in the face of teacher demands? Sitting still is not a behavior. You're asking him NOT to behave. Guess what, kids behave because they are alive, full of life and energy. What is he supposed to do with all of these demands to not behave? What am I as a parent being asked to do in this note from the teacher?

I let the teachers know that their instructions should be ACTIONS. If Forrest would have been told something active to do — *point at the basket you will shoot at* — he would do it enthusiastically and he (and the teacher) would have been fine.

The Ancestor Test forces us to consider what the person actually <u>did</u> when we notice the person failed to do something important. Perhaps during your observation homework you noticed that Brenda was not wearing her safety glasses at the beginning of her shift while she was testing adhesives. You wrote down: *Brenda was not wearing her safety glasses when testing.* I hope now you can apply the Ancestor Test and recognize that Brenda's great, great, great grandma is not wearing her safety glasses either. Instead, if we consider the active behavior Brenda did to BE in a state of unprotected eyes it will allow us to eventually find ways to get Brenda and other folks to wear their PPE.

To learn why, we need to talk to Brenda to discover the action that led her to forget her PPE. Perhaps we need to go back in time, even to the previous day, to find the critical behavior. Brenda would walk you through her end of shift routine: *"I get back to my locker and put all of my PPE together in one place. That way I have it all there the next shift and am more likely to remember everything."*

You found the action! *"Put all PPE in same place at end of shift so it's all together for the next shift and likely to be remembered."* Ancestors cannot place PPE together at the end of a shift. This action is a safe behavior because it makes Brenda more likely to wear her PPE the next day. Now that it's been described, you've learned a smart practice that you can teach to others. You'll find that when you ask, folks like Brenda are full of these safe habits.

But wait, you observed Brenda working without her safety glasses. What action was different this time that caused her to forget? Brenda reflects on the previous shift ending, *"As I recall, my supervisor called us into a meeting right after the shift to talk about our upcoming shut down. We went directly to the break room. We don't have to wear PPE in the break room so I think I probably put my safety glasses in my overalls."* Sure enough, she reaches into her lower pockets and pulls out the missing glasses.

Brenda still gave us a perfect behavioral description. *Put glasses in pocket instead of locker because of the unscheduled meeting.* This behavior, one that took place a day before, put her at risk the next shift. She had been taken out of her routine, put the glasses somewhere convenient, and, as a result, the glasses were not next to the rest of her PPE.

Because you can now describe the behavior in active (operational) terms you have a solution at your disposal: Allow workers to go back to their lockers and finish their routines before having them come to any end-of-shift meeting. In the meantime, take a picture of Brenda's locker with its organized PPE bundle to share with others.

We deal with "errors of omission" by hunting down the active behaviors that led up to the problem.

Brenda's actions give us an example of another behavioral truth that should be part of your rehab. Behavior doesn't occur in a vacuum; there is not only one option at a time. In fact, in any given situation, there are many different options for behaviors. At the end of her shift, Brenda could have asked the supervisor to give everyone a moment to go back to their lockers and arrange their PPE, she could have put all her loose PPE in her hair net, or she could have put her glasses in her pocket. Behaviors vary and in this variance there are behaviors that can put us at-risk and behaviors that keep us safe.

Your true risks lie in this behavioral variance. Behavioral variance drives up your injury rates. However, behavioral variance is also where your best opportunity for improvements is as well. Let's dive into that in the next chapter.

> Behaviors vary and in this variance there are behaviors that can put us at-risk and behaviors that keep us safe.

For now, practice your observations and descriptions of behavior. Get good at describing behavior; it is a functional practice that nurtures safety cultures. Get on with your REHAB!

~~DYSFUNCTIONAL~~ PRACTICE: LABEL THE BEHAVIOR

Approach behavior with the same unbiased analysis as scientists use with the elements of physics and chemistry. Behavior is neutral; it is not right or wrong, good or bad.

The properties of behavior make it particularly open to observation. First, behavior is omnipresent. Behaviors are prolific, visible (unlike attitudes, beliefs, values) and have an impact. All we need to do to change and improve is observable.

Approach any incident with a clear understanding of the cause and effect relationships between the behaviors related to the risk, and the reasons why that person, either knowingly (on purpose) or unknowingly found themselves in a position to take that risk.

Behaviors operate on their environment for a purpose. To describe behavior operationally, state the action, what is being operating on by the action, and why. No fluff, only what you can see.

CHAPTER 8:

Hacking Behaviors (in a good way)

Brenda, the one who left her safety glasses in her locker from the previous chapter, is a hacker. Not to be confused with a computer hacker; they have wreaked havoc on personal identities, bank accounts, computers, and even global affairs. Nope, Brenda is a behavior hacker (in a good way), and you should be too. Let me explain.

When we see Brenda wearing PPE we may be pleased she is protecting herself. But as we talk to her (remember that we are supposed to talk to our workers to understand the true causes of behavior), we begin to understand that she does a couple key things to achieve safe outcomes such as "wearing PPE." Indeed, to truly understand how to get desirable safety outcomes such as "PPE compliance," "using proper tools for the job," "organized housekeeping," "putting up a barrier," "preventive maintenance" and the like, we must first acknowledge that these safety outcomes result from a whole host of behaviors all conspiring to achieve the outcome we are looking for.

To wear PPE Brenda has a number of actions that she must perform successfully. Some she only has to do once in a while (e.g., "retrieve a new set of earplugs"); others she has to do daily (e.g., "retrieve PPE together from her locker at the beginning of the shift"); and still others are performed quite frequently (e.g., "insert earplugs into her ears after breaks"). Anything and everything that Brenda does that results in PPE use counts as a behavior we need to consider.

There's more to Brenda's story. Brenda designed strategies into her work environment to make wearing PPE more likely. She behaves in ways that structure her environment to prompt PPE wearing or make PPE wearing more convenient. Call her strategy, "self-managing." Workers do this a lot. We need to learn these self-managing behaviors from our workers and share them abundantly.

At the end of her shift Brenda takes off her PPE, cleans her protective gear, and arranges the many pieces of PPE sequentially on the shelf of her locker so they are available and clean for the next day. She ties the cord connecting her ear plugs to the strap of her work cap so they are always near her ears, making it less likely that she puts them down somewhere and loses them. The tethered earplugs are a prompt to remember to put them on.

I like calling Brenda's actions "Behavior Hacks" to sound cool to the millennials — all 83.1 million of them. For you old farts out there, to "hack" something is to take a short cut in a computer game or software that gets you to where you're going quicker and more pre-dictably. Merriam-Webster Dictionary defines a hack as "a creatively improvised solution…"

A Behavior Hacker like Brenda does the same thing. In fact, let's call it the "B-Hack" just to sound cooler.

Now there may be a dozen or so behaviors related to successful PPE use. Some are obvious parts of the sequence that everyone must do: "lifting ear plug to ear, insert, push." But B-Hacks are "creatively im-provised solutions" employees have adopted to manage their own environment so they achieve their safety outcomes more predictively every time.

If you asked experienced professionals like Brenda, and they thought about it a bit, they could easily list a number of B-Hacks that go into successful PPE use as well as most other safety outcomes. If you ask, you'll learn something about how front line people do their jobs using these B-Hacks. There are as many B-Hacks out there as there are workers.

Hacking is one of the main reasons you have so much variance across your workforce. You have workers who are always behaving to protect themselves and help others do the same. Alternatively, you also have workers who you always have to look out for (probably the newbies). Then you have everyone in between. The safest workers have the B-Hack strategies — and the best workers share the B-Hacks with others. The folks who are likely to get hurt? Well they have yet to find the optimal B-Hacks.

Learn this dear reader: you can only arrive at this level of selective and successful discrimination if you go ask the do-ers, the folks adding value and encountering hazards while doing the work. They are the ones who know the B-Hacks. They truly do, that's why they are so successful at keeping themselves safe.

A Behavior Hack (B-Hack) is a creatively improvised solution employees have adopted to manage their own environment so they achieve their safety outcomes more predictively every time.

As you continue your rehab away from labeling and going on fishing expeditions your next job is to go out and find a B-Hack. Choose a safety outcome, let's say "get the proper tool for the job," grab a couple of Brenda-types and start asking questions.

• **How do they prompt themselves — self manage — to get the proper tool at the beginning of the task?**

• **How do they make the proper tools more convenient?**

And the most important question:

• **How can we ensure they always have the proper tool?**

So go out and find the B-Hacks … go ahead, I'll be here when you get back… Tick…tock…tick…no seriously, put down this book and go do your homework!

Did you find some B-Hacks? If not then re-read my chapters on fear and hiding behaviors and go back out and try again.

If you did find a B-Hack or two you'll discover the best Hacks don't occur during the task itself, they tend to occur: a) in the intervals between tasks or shifts; and b) they occur with other people's help. Indeed, many B-Hacks involve asking someone else to check your work or observe your behaviors (one of the scientific tactics behind behavioral safety programs).

Hack your Training

Now let's look at Behavior Hacking in your training. Consider when you train your newbies, or retrain your oldies. In the training you probably address the tasks they will be doing on the job and the things they should do to keep safe. "OK newbies, here is your testing table where you will evaluate samples of the adhesives we are putting on the product. This is a loud environment and you will be working with chemicals. Therefore, you need to wear earplugs, chemical-resistant clothing and gloves, and safety goggles."

Nice exhortation. Certainly, all the newbies are willing workers and want to stay safe so they will endeavor to wear the required PPE. Yet you find they don't follow through. Hopefully by this point in your rehab you don't label them as stupid, get upset and insert fear during your fishing trips.

Instead you have the urge to retrain, perhaps disguised as coaching: "You need to wear your earplugs, gloves, and goggles." This is really just another way of calling them stupid, right? Might as well say *"You're so dim-witted I need to retell you the obvious."* Here's what happened. Your training did not give the newbie the ability to <u>discriminate</u> the behaviors they need to achieve consistent PPE wearing. Let's define discriminate in psychological terms: *Discrimination is the ability to perceive and respond to different stimuli in the environment with the appropriate behavior(s).* In too many training classes, workers are lectured on the desired outcome ("Wear your PPE;" "Don't mix these chemicals;" "Stay out of the line of fire") while the actual behaviors needed to help workers achieve these outcomes are rarely discussed, especially those B-Hacks that your best workers engage in strategically. Your best and safest workers like Brenda have discriminated (perceived and selected) the behaviors related to successful PPE use; your training didn't.

So let's redesign your training to discriminate, shall we? Successful training meets the needs of your workers. Let me offer this:

A. Your workers need to discriminate the B-Hacks.

The best practice is to have sessions where workers talk to each other about the various B-Hacks they have adopted. Then encourage your workers to adopt them as standard work practices (heck, you should even revise those operating procedures, JSAs, and observation forms to design in these B-Hacks).

B. Your workers need to practice the B-Hacks.

This important step is often neglected. Encourage your workers to try out the new behaviors, ask workers to observe each other and provide each other feedback until everyone is at 100-percent B-Hack effectiveness.

C. Repeat until this is ingrained in how they work as a team.

This ongoing process would make an awesome beginning for a shift toolbox talk, right?

This is also why on-the-job training with a mentor can be a good idea, but *only if* that mentor is one of those folks with a repertoire of their own B-Hacks. They can help the newbie discriminate, allow the newbie to practice, and give the newbie feedback to achieve fluency (meaning: faster mental processing of what needs to be done correctly).

(Have you noticed that we haven't been in a classroom at all?)

Discrimination is the best Safety Rule

Discrimination is a key behavioral science principle. Not the type of discrimination that plagues racial relations; no, it is the type of discrimination that allows you to decipher the right behavior for the right situation at the right moment. Your workers should discriminate between the behaviors that can get them hurt and the ones that will keep them safe.

Remember that in behavioral science we call behaviors "operants." We use this term because when we behave what we are doing is "operating" on the environment in response to a certain stimulus. And the reason we operate on the environment is to get some outcome, as a consequence of our behavior. Your phone buzzes, you behave by pulling the phone out of your pocket. You operated on the stimulus in your surrounding environment and your behavior produced the opportunity to talk to your friend about your new smoker (the consequence). Your experience with that stimulus in your environment (the pone buzzing in your pocket) helped you discriminate when to pull your phone out of your pocket.

Discrimination is something you do when making a decision. Scientists also think it's part of your automatic processing; something that happens pre-consciousness Discrimination of this sort can be summarized in a three-part sentence, what scientists call a **Rule:**

> **"In this situation...**
> **If I act this way...**
> **Then this will happen."**

Consider this example from the oil and gas industry. A field operator, Sam, is fixing some piping using clamps and other tools. He finds himself with a clamp that is slightly larger than the coil. Sam must decide if he should rig the clamp so it fits. So he says to himself:

In this situation...
"Hmmm...The correct size clamp is back in supply truck and our client is demanding to get the job done by noon..."

If I act this way...
"So, if I simply modify this available clamp on this casing..."

Then this will happen
"Then I'll get the job done quicker and keep my supervisor off my case."

However, rigging the wrong-sized clamp might also result in the casing eventually bursting. *"Then the casing could burst and cause a release of chemicals... and someone could get hurt"* (then this will happen). The field operator might also get disciplined for non-conformance to the SOP. *"Then I could lose my job"* (then this will happen)!

Yes, all these consequences could happen... so how does Sam discriminate between these options?

I told you behavior doesn't happen in a vacuum. Behaviors occur within time; it takes time to behave. Moreover, behaviors are happening all the time for a variety of reasons. Behaviors compete for time. Certainly, Sam could intentionally discriminate the actions to secure the casing safely by walking to the supply truck and retrieving the correct size clamp. Alternatively, Sam could engage in the riskier option by intentionally discriminating the actions to secure the casing with the available clamp. He couldn't do both at the same time. Sam has to discriminate between competing behaviors, both with different outcomes to consider.

Sam compares his options. For one option, he would follow the operating procedures and, according to the engineers, prevent the casing from failing. With the other option, the job will most certainly get done quicker; that's a good thing for him, his work crew and his bosses. However, his risk-taking in this option could cause an incident. To be sure, it is unlikely the case will burst if he modifies the clamp to fit, and it's rare to get caught and written up. Sam knows this because he's seen others use the wrong tool, even the wrong clamp and nothing ever happened… shoot, he had probably used the available tool in the past and nothing happened. Double-shoot, if he got caught his supervisor probably would not write him up for using the wrong tool because Sam was getting the job done faster, something that benefits the supervisor. The bad consequences were not likely outcomes. Because of the "git 'er done" situation Sam found himself in, and the rule that he calculated, rigging the clamp to fit the casing ended up being the risky way to go… and on he went.

Think of behavior like flowing water. Water follows the banks of a river. The banks of a river direct the water to turn this way and that. Behavior follows the path of least resistance. The situation surrounding Sam's work is akin to the banks of the river. This situation creates the channels that form the banks that guide his behavior. The lack of the available tool, the pressure from leadership to be quick, and other workers modeling short cuts guided his behavior just like the banks of a river guide water downstream.

In this Situation…

A situation or context that directs behavior is called the "antecedent" by scientists. The term originates all the way back to Latin meaning to "go before." Antecedents happen prior to behavior. Therefore, antecedents are present when the behavior happens and provide us with all the clues needed to discriminate. We're informed when it is the best time to execute a behavior, or not to.

I was in Mexico, where some Spanish-speaking managers told me the word "antecedent" also refers to "past experience." I liked that nuance. An antecedent is the situation we find ourselves in that help us discriminate, based on past experience, if it is the right time to perform a behavior.

In the safety world we use a lot of antecedents that guide safe behavior. We train, we provide instructions, we put up signage, supervisors direct, and safety meetings inform. If we fail to provide adequate antecedents, behavior will go anywhere that ensures the path of least resistance, like water that jumps its banks. When behavior is not discriminated an employee just wings it. An untrained employee will behave all over the map. Our training should help discriminate the right behaviors for the specific tasks to keep workers safe. Training directs behavior.

There are always competing antecedents. You can have all the training, instructions, and signage you want, but you will also have time pressure during upsets, inadequate tools or equipment, and peers who teach us short cuts (just to name a few competing antecedents). This competition can direct a worker to perform at-risk behavior.

Sam's antecedents presented him with this situation: he didn't have the right tool; it was back in the supply truck. His work needed to get done by noon. He had also been trained to determine the correct casing for the job and we "assume" he has read the 30-page Standard Operating Procedure (SOP L3424C Rev16.4) clearly listing the casings, tools, and processes. So which behavioral channel does he follow?

Well, which channel does a river follow when banks overflow? Water follows the channel that has the steepest downward slope. Certainly you've been at the beach and built a sand castle at one point in your life, at least I hope you've had the pleasure. The best castle builders create a moat around the castle. How do you do that? You dig a trench around the castle with a slope steeper than the sand progressing back to the surf. When a wave reaches your moat, the water will follow the steeper slope around your castle and your castle is protected from assault... until the tide comes in.

Sam is confronted with two channels enticing his behavior based on the antecedents of his situation. These antecedents only *direct* or *channel* behavior, they don't *motivate* behavior. This is important. *What motivates behavior is what happens after behavior, as a consequence of the behavior.* If the consequence of rigging the clamp is going to be getting in trouble with the boss, then that channel's slope will be pretty shallow because there is a slim-to-none chance of that happening since the boss is sitting comfortably in the air-conditioned trailer and not watching. Sam would not be motivated by that unlikely consequence of getting in trouble. On the other hand, if antecedents are telling Sam that he must be done by noon, then any behaviors (e.g., rigging an incorrect clamp) that save time will have the steepest grade, the easiest path to follow, and it will motivate behavior.

The steeper grade the faster the water will flow. The faster water flows the more likely it is to carve out new and stronger banks. Anyone who has been in a torrential downpour can see how a deluge of water can carve little gorges in dirt as rain rushes downhill. These gorges can determine the direction of water in the future. I live in the mountains; my downhill neighbors own a cabin right next to a creek fed by springs high above us on Rich Mountain. The banks of that creek are fairly deep from years of shuttling spring water and rain. However, after a particularly strong rain the creek jumped its banks right beside the cabin and created a new channel right into their foundation. Until they got a track hoe down there and repaired the bank, the new channel kept feeding the creek into their house, destabilizing the cabin and flooding the yard.

You may have your antecedents, your riverbanks, neatly arranged with your SOPs, training, and the like. However, stronger consequences, like time pressure, can make behavior "jump the banks" and carve new paths. And those new paths may be risky. As behavior follows strong consequences, antecedents related to those consequences get stronger at helping your workers discriminate at-risk behavior.

Sam not only rigs incorrect clamps when he is under time pressure... it just becomes how he does his job. He searches for short cuts any time he can — he creates his own B-Hacks, not for safety's sake, but for other purposes. Sam's behavior has been discriminated, for better or worse. Those risky channels have been cut deep, pulling other behaviors to it.

...then this will happen

In previous chapters, if you did your homework, you went out to observe and you "pinpointed" behaviors that may put your workers at-risk or help them stay safe. When a worker is in-the-moment, they go through the quick mental process of discriminating the right behavior to engage in depending on the situation.

Sam, for example, does his own pinpointing: *"...if I act this way."* As we discussed, safe behavior doesn't occur in a vacuum; Sam has a number of options for his behavior. He can stop what he is doing, go to the supply truck and retrieve the correct-sized clamp for the casing. Or he can do some on-the-spot fabrication to rig the slightly larger clamp to fit. As he goes through this process of discrimination he will be motivated to act one way or the other.

Central question: *What motivates behavior?* In behavior science we are fond of reciting a simple yet profound truth:

consequences choose the behavior.

Some consequences we call "appetitive." This means the person behaving has an appetite for the consequence. If you have a hunger for something you are motivated to go get it and consume whatever it is. Perhaps you're a bit hungry and find yourself with an appetite for burgers. Are you motivated to go to the burger joint up the street from the plant? Perhaps you have an appetite for some social time with a friend so you invite her to go with you. You do these things and, as a consequence of your behavior, you find yourself eating a burger and laughing with a friend.

You have now experienced the consequence and you find it yummy and fun. So much so that you want to do it again when you have another opportunity *...in this situation...* where you're working at the plant and you and your friend have some free time at lunch. Your behavior was *reinforced* by this consequence and, when the situation arises, those consequences will choose those behaviors again and off you go to the burger joint.

Which of Sam's behavioral choices will be reinforced by an appetitive consequence? What does Sam hunger for? Well, let's check out his situation, the antecedents, to determine what he will discriminate as the best choice for him. He and his team have an appetite to get the work done by noon, so getting the work done sooner is yummy. This motivation to get the work done sooner helps Sam discriminate that rigging the clamp is the best way to go.

Other consequences may be considered "aversive." The term "aversion" comes from Latin origins in which ancient Romans defined "aversion" as *"turn away."* A modern definition would say that something aversive is a "turn off" or "distasteful," which brings us back to appetite, except this is the opposite of hungering for something appealing. Aversive consequences are ones we try to turn away from because they are yucky to us.

Perhaps you've waited for the weekend to mow your lawn, an activity you actually enjoy normally because of the exercise and fresh air. However, when Saturday arrives the sky opens up and sheets of rain start falling... *in this situation.* Mowing ...*if I act this way...* will result in you getting drenched, your mower getting water in the carbure-tor, and grass clumping up in your blades ...*then this will happen.* Are you motivated to go out and mow? In the past, mowing-in-the-rain behavior was probably *punished* by coming in contact with the negative consequences and so you are less likely to mow in the rain anytime in the future. These consequences don't lead you to choose mowing; instead they choose college football sitting in your dry den.

Which of Sam's behavioral choices would be punished by an aversive consequence? His antecedents tell us that the correct clamp was back at the supply truck ...*In this situation.* For Sam to use the correct-sized clamp ...*if I act this way...* he would have to stop work, interrupting the flow of work by others, to walk over to the supply truck, deal with the cranky supply manager, and most likely come back to a cranky su-pervisor miffed at Sam leaving his task ...*then this will happen.* Getting the correct-sized clamp would be quite yucky — aversive — for Sam. He probably experienced the bad taste in his mouth the first time he fetched a missing tool in the middle of a task, so now he turns away from that unappetizing consequence.

Hold up! Couldn't an aversive consequence happen as a result of Sam's using-the-wrong-clamp behavior? Isn't the clamp more likely to bust, releasing the hose's chemicals and possibly injuring someone? Wouldn't these aversive outcomes punish the behavior of rigging the incorrect-sized clamp (choosing the step ladder over the six-foot ladder... taking off the guard to clean the loom... pulling off the glove to get a better feel for the wires... skipping some preventive maintenance steps... driving in excess of the plant's speed limit... etc... etc)?

True, these outcomes are potentially punishing consequences. As we have noted, that there are often multiple consequences for a behavior. Rigging the incorrect clamp concurrently helps Sam avoid all the effort and bother of getting the correct clamp <u>and</u> puts him and his fellow roustabouts at risk of a high-pressure release.

> **In this situation...**
> *The correct size clamp is back in the supply truck and our client is demanding to get the job done by noon;*
>
> **If I act this way...**
> *use the available clamp;*
>
> **Then, this will happen...**
> *Then I'll get the job done quicker, allowing others to do their job, and get keep my supervisor off my case by completing the job by noon.*
>
> **But, this could happen too...**
> *The rigged clamp could explode, sending chemicals into our workspace at high pressure hurting or killing anyone around.*

We now know the behavior options facing Sam. We know there are a couple different possible consequences for the at-risk behavior of rigging the clamp. These consequences conflict. Which one will be more likely to motivate his behavior? The consequence that is more POWERFUL.

Power-up your Consequences

Any consequence that is more PROMPT, PROBABLE, and PERSONAL is more powerful. For you engineers out there, I give you the POWER QUOTIENT:

$$POWER = f(P^3)$$

The power of a consequence to motivate a behavior is a function (f) of these three Ps.

PROMPT: Consequences that happen right away are more powerful than those that are delayed. We tend to choose behaviors that provide immediate consequences.

My iPad games offer immediate (and abundant) reinforcement. When I win a round I immediately move up a level and get new exciting opportunities. In contrast, reinforcement for writing this book is quite delayed. In fact, as I write this, I have yet to come in contact with any reinforcement at all for all my keyboard tapping. No one has bought the book, read it, talked to me about it. The reinforcement for writing is quite delayed. Guess which behavior won out as I drank my coffee this morning, the iPad game or writing?

It is hard to delay reinforcement. In fact, one of the signs of cognitive development in toddlers is if they can delay reinforcement. Put a cookie in front of a two-year-old; they will be quite pleased and want to eat it (we all would). Then tell them you are going to leave the room for ten minutes and if the cookie is still there when you return, they will be rewarded with a second cookie. Their face will show excitement for the prospect of a second cookie. However, you will see quite a different face when you return after your ten-minute interval. Their face will now show the crumbs of what used to be the original cookie and a look of disappointment in their loss of a second cookie.

Give the same setup to a three-year-old. You'll see him or her reach for the cookie and fight their hand away as they deny the immediate reinforcement in favor of the slightly delayed reinforcer. Jumping 50 years into the future, and now a fifty-four-year-old plays games on his iPad attaining the immediate reinforcement it offers instead of tapping on his keyboard. Indeed, delaying reinforcement is a sign of intelligence in kids... and adults. Think about it: college is a long exercise in delaying reinforcement! Most good-paying jobs are as well.

Let's face it, we all are humans (presumably) and behave in ways that provide for prompt consequences. Smoking and other drugs are the poster children for immediate appetitive consequences paired with delayed aversive consequences. Smoking will decrease your life and make your final years less healthy, yet those delayed consequences pale when the nicotine feels good right now. This is why ergonomic behaviors are so hard to encourage. The price I have to pay for slouching at my desk, or bending at the waist, or wearing flip flops will not be realized until years later when my neck, lower back, and plantar tendons in my feet ache (I'm in my 50s now so I've discovered those consequences).

Indeed, musculoskeletal disorders are a very delayed consequence of many work (and play) behaviors. Because they are so delayed, the power of these achy consequences to discourage our slouching, bending, twisting, and pulling at work is weak. So we engage in ergonomically risky behaviors for years without consequence. Rest assured, they'll get you in time.

But wait! It is also true that your behaviors can hurt you immediately. When you get injured it typically happens right away. Our manager could have fallen immediately as a consequence of standing on the top of the step ladder, right? Wouldn't that immediate aversive consequence satisfy the prompt portion of the power quotient? Wouldn't the prospect of immediately getting hurt motivate the safe alternative? The answer comes down to that very word: "prospect" — there is a potential or likelihood but there is also a potential or likelihood the consequence doesn't happen. The consequence also needs to be Probable.

PROBABLE: Consequences more certain to happen will be more powerful than those less certain to happen. This principle is at the heart of choices we make in risk-taking, safety, investments and relationships.

Let's face it, the behaviors we engage in to stay safe protect us against the improbable chance that we may get hurt. Similarly, when we take a safety shortcut, we do so against the improbable risk of something going wrong and getting injured.

This is why we call behaviors "at-risk" instead of "unsafe." These behaviors cause risk but not certain injury. In fact, the probability of injury, for the manager using the step ladder, for the supervisor who skips the pressure check, and for Sam rigging the casing, is usually very low. In contrast, at-risk behavior usually is associated with very probable appetitive consequences that are more convenient, comfortable, or productive. The desirable consequences of taking the risk are much more probable (and prompt) than the possible, but improbable consequence of injury.

Nearly all our decisions are a risk/reward scenario; think back to risk-taking, investments and relationships. The risk/reward ratio isn't only calculated by workers. Leaders, whose job it is to make decisions, face safety decisions all the time and risk/reward probability is a major factor in these decisions.

I recall having a conversation with a managing director for one of the largest open pit precious metal mines in the world. It is so big you can see it from space (or Google Earth). I stood at the edge of the mine and the ledges were too many to count as I looked at the pit some 2,500 feet deep. Some ledges had failed and you could see slide debris covering hundreds of feet on the wall through which new roads had to be cut. You could not see the men at the bottom and the distance relegated huge haul trucks into ants.

What struck me was how small the floor of the pit was and how steep the walls had become. When we talked with the managing director he described his dilemma. The managing director knew a valuable lode of ore extended a couple hundred feet beneath the pit floor. It was right there. To get to it they had to dig deeper. This would inevitably lengthen and steepen the walls, a dangerous tempt of fate. To make the mine safer, however, they would have to start digging way up at the top to widen the pit many hundreds of feet, creating larger, less steep ledges as they dug back down to the floor. This would cost months of productivity at a couple hundred thousand dollars a day, in addition to the significant capital to invest in widening the pit.

I didn't envy his dilemma. To make the decision more high stakes, the mine had experienced a fatality in the previous year from a slide. I knew the certainty of losing all that money was much more probable than another killer slide.

This scenario is repeated over and over for leaders in heavy industry, oil and gas, transportation, and many other fields. The cost of keeping downward pressure and using different cement on the Deepwater Horizon well was a million dollars a day in lost revenue and capital. This was certain; the chance of a blowout, less so. Not in this case... resulting in the loss of 11 lives and the livelihood of millions of Gulf residents (and billions in fines and restitution).

To further complicate matters, most workers never experience the negative consequence of a serious injury, either to themselves or co-workers. You can go an entire career without experiencing this conse-quence. A central scientific principle: a behavior must come in contact with the consequence in order to be reinforced or punished. In the absence of this experience there can be no learning. We call this the "avoidance paradox." How do we learn to avoid negative outcomes, like injuries, if we never experience them?

I've seen many safety managers try to make the consequences of safety performance probable by rewarding workers with trinkets such as jackets or with pizza parties. This is fallacy. Is the fact they didn't get hurt not a sufficient enough reward! Does everyone need a new jacket to motivate them to stay safe? Would this break through the avoidance paradox? Work safe for the new jacket — now that's what

I call a paradox! So employees are not supposed to work safe when a new jacket is not on the table? Fortunately, we learn how to apply the brakes at stop lights without having to experience driving into an intersection, getting into a wreck, and getting injured (like I tried to do at the beginning of this book).

Humans' ability to discriminate choices and play out the probability of consequences in our heads is exceptional... world class... the reason why we rule the planet. We can do this because the human brain is particularly adept at allocating a lot of neural space to bits of information that are personal and meaningful to us. For example, we are much more likely to remember events that happen to us rather than to other people. Similarly, we remember information better if we can relate it to our lives. Thus, consequences are more powerful if they are personal. The behavioral programming that goes into our safety management systems must take advantage of this. This brings us to our third "P"'

PERSONAL: Consequences that are significant to us personally are more powerful than consequences that don't have much personal impact. This factor is harder to put your finger on because there is variability across people as to what consequences they find personally significant.

Many intricacies go into this. First, there are differences in what each of us value as a personal reinforcing consequence. Then we are constantly trying to figure out what 100+ workers all find personally significant. Don't go down that road.

I've seen many safety campaigns emphasize the personal significance of the consequences of injury by putting up posters showing workers' children with the caption: "The reason you're working is to bring home money for your family. Work to avoid injuries so you can help them enjoy it." It's a very powerful message that can work wonders. I remember once chatting with a guy who didn't have a family yet and was working to make money for a new truck. Let's not assume we know what consequences will be personally reinforcing to folks.

Further, what was reinforcing in the past may be less reinforcing now because we get satiated. My raving about my friend's banana pudding reinforces me with more delicious banana pudding. If I get banana pudding each time I see her, my raving will calm down. There is only so much banana pudding a man can eat. How many company shirts does a person really need? In contrast, when we've been deprived of some consequences, they become more reinforcing. My friend moved away... I'll do anything for her banana pudding!

Finally, what helps the community or organization may not be personally significant to us. If we all could relate to the common good we'd not have to fight so hard to get people to recycle, give to charity, improve the quality of their work to combat customer complaints, and say something to the fellow worker who seems to always take the short cut and not check the hose pressure before decoupling. In this last case, and in many, many other cases, caring for the other person who may get hurt is superseded by the personal significance of maintaining enjoyable personal relationships. Telling someone they are doing wrong can turn the whole crew against you. Social reinforcers are a very strong personally significant consequence, one that overpowers many others.

And this is where we can influence Sam! We know very well from our discussion that safety is a fight with human nature. At-risk behaviors typically have more Ps in the P^3 quotient. The appetitive consequences of taking risks happen more *promptly* and *predictably* because they are typically more convenient, less cumbersome, and quicker than the safe alternative. But humans have huge brains, allocating a lot of mental capacity to personally significant information, especially if the data have to do with our social life. This we can hack!

Hack-It!

Reading this far into this book, you know the odds are against safety. You know consequences stack the odds against safety because many safety acts are inconvenient, slow, and cumbersome, and the chances of injury low.

So it's time to ask Brenda for advice. Brenda puts all her PPE in an organized pile in her locker so it is promptly ready for her in the morning with high probability. Through this simple B-Hack, the act of putting on PPE becomes less punishing. It's organized, accessible, ready to go. One set of Brenda's behaviors makes the second set of behaviors more likely to happen. And, the fact that she came up with this B-Hack makes it personal to her. She's achieved her P^3 quotient.

B-Hacks are the behaviors that workers have adopted to MAKE CERTAIN they are put in a position NOT to take the risk. If we can discover these *behaviors behind the behaviors* that make us safe we beat the odds. These B-Hacks take advantage of the P^3 quotient instead of being a slave to it. B-Hacks make the consequences of safe behavior more prompt, probable, and personal by making the behaviors more convenient, less cumbersome and quicker.

What to do about Sam? What B-Hack will make him less likely to rig an oversized clamp? We know the consequences are against the safe behavior of going back to the supply truck because this extra work and extra time is punishing. What behavior can Sam do *beforehand* to make certain he does not find himself in a position to take that risk? If you can't figure it out, go ask Sam. He will point out pre-task procedures he could to double check specs and tools needed. He may over-stock his crew's tool crib.

> B-Hacks make the consequences of safe behavior more prompt, probable, and personal by making the behaviors more convenient, less cumbersome and quicker.

Better yet, Sam can get his crew together and have them brainstorm B-Hacks to manipulate the 3Ps in safety's favor. Especially the last one — personal.

Remember our definition of safety culture? Safety culture is people talking to each other about safety. If Sam and his co-workers have a culture of talking about safety, then we have created the best hack of all, folks. The Safety Culture Hack. Even if managers let Sam down by adopting a schedule to rush his work, even if the supply chief let Sam down by giving him the wrong clamps, even if Sam let himself down by succumbing to his situation... even if everything puts Sam in the position to take the risk... who is working right next to him?

If you have a culture of talking about safety then your fellow workers will be, well... talking about safety.

> *"Sam, what task you got going on this morning? Have you checked the specs for the clamps?..."*
>
> *"Sam, go on to the next clamp for the time being, I've got a break so I'll go get you the right clamp for that hose..."*
>
> *"Let me talk to the supervisor about the noon deadline, better to get it right than fast."*

Hacked! A safety culture of workers talking to other workers, looking out for each other, and not letting a fellow worker find themselves in the position to take the risk is the greatest B-Hack of all.

Unless you are still addicted to the dysfunctional practices that kill safety cultures.

~~DYS~~FUNCTIONAL PRACTICE: DISCRIMINATE BEHAVIORS

Behavior Hacks are "creatively improvised solutions" employees have adopted to manage their own environment so they achieve their safety outcomes more predictively every time. Ask your workers to find out how they achieve this.

Training must give workers the ability to perceive the appropriate cues in their work environment and discriminate the appropriate behavior to engage. Good discrimination allows workers to verbalize the rule: **"In this situation... If I act this way ... Then this will happen."**

Consequences choose the behavior. Any consequence that is more PROMPT, PROBABLE, and PERSONAL is more powerful at motivating a behavior.

Most workers never experience the negative consequence of a serious injury, either to themselves or co-workers. Behavior must come in contact with the consequence in order to be reinforced or punished. In many cases threat of injury will not maintain safe behavior.

A safety culture of workers talking to other workers, looking out for each other, and not letting a fellow worker take the risk is the strongest consequence motivating safety behavior (and the cheapest).

CHAPTER 9:
Learn instead of Label

NOW LISTEN CAREFULLY: your system is perfectly designed to get the results you received because your system is perfectly designed to produce the behaviors you shaped.

You built it, folks. You and your engineers, and your managers, and your industry egg-heads, and your consultants, and people you'll never know who built parts of your system long ago. All of you constructed the situation. Don't go blame the worker. Instead, work with that worker to understand why, in the situations you built, they felt the risk was necessary; why perhaps, they weren't aware of the risk at all. Feeling a lot of responsibility now?

This maxim can be liberating. You can't fix stupid. You can't fix labels that you mistakenly apply when you don't understand the influence of your system. However, you can fix the system, sometimes by yourself, sometimes with a lot of help. The system is under your control.

This approach opens us up to a wide range of possibilities, a wide range of things we call "solutions." Have you heard of these? Solutions are functional. Solutions are practical. Solutions are what we seek. They displace the need to blame and label people — dysfunctional practices that lead to fear and avoidance. Instead we seek to engage in the <u>functional</u> practice of seeking solutions.

A Game of Dominoes

My mom grew up in Texas. The game in her family was dominoes. When I visited as a lad, Grandpa would come home from a day at the ranch, grab a beer, and play dominoes with Grandma, Mom and Dad. I remember his large hands holding all seven dominoes in one grip as they played Texas 42. It's a classic game, the teamwork engaging, and the strategy challenging. Of course, us kids were not allowed to play. So we devised our own game… one made up by generations of kids. I bet you played it too.

My brothers and I would line up the porcelain domino tiles optimally an inch apart. We would try to line up as many as possible in as many interesting patterns as we could. With sensitive, surgical hands we tried to set each domino perilously close to the existing row without bumping the nearby standing domino. Doing so would send the other 20+ dominoes cascading down. We had to get it perfect. There are 28 dominoes in a pack, the best we achieved, as I recall, was three full packs all lined up ready to go.

For the grand finale, we would gently push the first domino toward the line and watch the kinetic power as one domino tipped into the next and the next and the next in a cacophony of cause and effect motions.

H.W. Heinrich (1886-1962) asserted nearly 80 years ago that 88 percent of worker injuries are due to the worker's unsafe act. He proposed a model using cascading dominos that suggested the worker's ancestry and social upbringing (first domino) led to being at fault (second) which led to an unsafe act (third) which led to accident (forth) and injuries (the last domino to fall). Heinrich was an insurance investigator. He certainly didn't understand behavior. In my opinion, he blamed workers for injuries and slapped a label on them in his definition of the first domino.

It is easy to see how Heinrich arrived at this theory. When a human interacts with a hazardous situation, behavior is typically the last thing to occur before things go wrong. It is almost a requirement for an injury.

The safest thing for a human to do is nothing — like a dead ancestor. Work is active. It involves behaviors happening in the midst of hazards.

Sure, 88 percent of the time a behavior could be observed before an unfortunate and possibly injurious event. But to analyze behaviors as the *cause* of the injury leads us to blaming and labeling. This is one of the serious safety practice dysfunctions we've been talking about throughout this book.

Heinrich's publications popularized an insidious trend of "blame the worker." It is this message that kills trust, engagement, communication and safety cultures. Beginning eight decades ago, all investigations, analyses, and communications lead to the conclusion that small and large incidents alike are due, 88 percent of the time, to "Human Error" — translation: "Stupid Human."

We now know the chilling effect of this time-worn message. Employees avoided reporting safety issues and incidents for fear of being lumped into that 88 percent. Now we know better. We know the blinding, stifling effect that the "88 percent human error" had on root cause analyses. Investigations (and insight) stopped due to the 88 percent human failure assumption. Analyses became less equipped to deliver a solution other than somehow changing something in the stupid person at fault. We got training and more training, and discipline and more discipline. But really, you can't fix stupid and no one is stupid.

Somehow Heinrich's stat has been attached like a yoke around behavior-based safety (BBS) programs by groups like the United Auto Workers. Remember that Heinrich's third domino in his theory pointed to human behavior that was "unsafe." It seems all attempts, scientific or otherwise, to analyze and influence the causes of behavior get a bad rap. This has had unfortunate consequences. Behavioral programs have been damned for blaming the worker when in fact they do just the opposite.

If you know behavior science you know we follow the works of B.F. Skinner and W. Edwards Deming; not Heinrich. Behavioral science always looks at environmental influences on behavior and never blames the worker as the root cause. Instead, we see behavior as a result of other causes.

I introduced W. Edwards Deming (1900-1993) to you in previous chapters. Like Heinrich, he was a statistician who spent his career trying to understand the variance that leads to errors. His focus was to protect the quality of products and services in our economy. From his analyses, Deming concluded something very different than Heinrich. Deming did agree that most errors are associated to human behavior — BUT he went on to conclude that 94 percent of human behavior is due to the system that caused it. Skinner and us behavioral scientists would fully agree.

That leaves a small percentage of human behavior occurring due to person factors such as personality (labels). I think we made the case in previous chapters that us humans are notoriously bad at accurately labeling someone's person factors based on our flawed, biased attributions. We also made the case that it is notoriously hard to change a person. I have clinical psychology colleagues who go through intense university training for nine years and still have a challenging time helping people change — by so-called "getting into their heads." So, when it comes to safety, I'd rather work with the 94 percent of behavior I can change than the six percent of behavior based on person factors that I probably can't get at.

What is this "system" Deming talked about?

Everything that can influence behavior, and that's a lot, is part of this system. Let's start with all of the things managers do (or don't do) to help their employees stay safe. This would include making safety budget investments and training, mentoring, policies, procedures, safety processes like Job Safety Audits (JSA), inspections, reporting schemes for close calls and minor injuries, meetings (upon meetings upon meetings), signage, discipline and justice, incentives, awareness programs, and the list goes on. The system also includes the tools available to use, the equipment to be worked with, and the facilities to be worked in — and all the engineering designs and plans that go into them. Preventive maintenance, warehousing the proper replacements, availability and suitability of personal protective equipment all count as system factors. The work process itself is important, as are production expectations/quotas and the bonuses tied to them. Supervision and leadership behaviors are huge system factors as they are they are often the precursor to the rest of this stuff.

There are many more system factors out there; I could write a whole chapter on them. Unfortunately, without a sober analysis of the causes of behavior, you may never learn what the precursors are in your situation. If you insist on blaming the worker you won't find deeper causes and those system factors will be still out there, lurking, ready to steer the next worker, like the banks of a river, toward the next risk.

Who sets up this system? We all do. Leaders build it when their behavior (leaders behave too) sets in motion the creation and adaptation of systems (that's why you need to pass on this book to your leaders when you're done). Supervisors and engineers and planners build smaller pieces and maintain these systems. Other contributors include the different support functions such as HR and its policies, finance and those bean counters, maintenance, facilities management, procurement, and contracting, to name a few — all those folks in offices whose decisions and actions have direct or indirect impact on the context within which your workers work.

I'm not done. Governmental regulatory actions contribute to the system as do your competitors' actions, the local economy, and your industry trade groups out there disseminating best practices. Your suppliers, expert solution provider consultants, knowledge givers (yours truly), insurance companies are all potential influencers. Your stakeholders (demanding stockholders and customers) and owners and financiers and board certainly can have an impact on the systems that shape behavior. All beyond your pay grade perhaps.

Complex right? See why it is sooooooo easy to blame just one person instead? Blaming one person for errors is low-hanging fruit. The path of least resistance. Much easier than pulling back the layers of a complex system that actually caused the problem. We need a crystal ball that helps us learn what system factors are at play so we can surgically make the correct changes to make a difference. Fortunately, we have that crystal ball.

A Different Domino Theory

Consider your last injury, one where it seemed the person hurt was at fault. Let's not ask the question why the worker was stupid enough to take the risk. Let's instead ask the why the worker took the risk in the first place. Instead of seeing behavior as the cause of the injury, let's examine what caused the behavior. What system factors failed the worker so the worker, knowingly or unknowingly, was put in a position to take the risk.

I just learned last week from a client about a young man who was badly injured at a South American mine. There was an oil leak on a processing unit and this maintenance worker was asked to go fix it. The way the unit was designed (a system factor) required him to climb the unit and look over an edge to see the leak. He powered down the machine and locked out. However, the leak did not produce when the machine was not running. So the young man climbed back down, powered up the machine, and then climbed back up to witness the leak. Moving to get a better angle and reaching his arm to remove some debris exposed him to an oncoming blade which severed his arm and threw him to the ground below.

The young man admits he left the machine running to better get a look at the leak. He knew the danger of putting his arm into the machine but thought he timed his reach to avoid the slow moving blade. He miscalculated and his arm was amputated. Do we blame the human factor? Human error? Stupidity? It was easy for even the young man to blame himself.

Blaming the injured does not solve the problem, nor does it help us avoid risk and injury in the future. Human behavior is not the cause of injuries; at-risk behavior results from other factors, such as the design of machinery, the layout of work space, inaccessibility of tools and PPE, decisions to rush production, and so on.

Let's consider a different Cascading Dominoes Theory to describe the real cause and effect relationship between behaviors and injuries.

There are dominoes other than the ones Heinrich proposed, cascading *well before* the behavior, setting the context for the worker, either knowingly or unknowingly, to be in the position to take a risk. Physics and chemistry then take over on unfortunate, yet thankfully sporadic occasions, and injury occurs.

Let's make the implications of a systems approach crystal clear: your system is perfectly designed to get the behaviors that it shapes. This means your system is perfectly designed for the worker to take a risk. And here is the sobering conclusion: Your system is perfectly designed to produce the injuries you've suffered.

> Your system is perfectly designed to get the behaviors that it shapes. This means your system is perfectly designed for the worker to take a risk. Thus, your system is perfectly designed to produce the injuries you've suffered.

When we fail to set up the right system we create a cascade of causes ready to fall, like dominoes; if they line up just right, risks are taken and injuries occur. Our young maintenance man's behavior was the last domino to fall before he got caught in the machine and had his life changed forever. What dominoes fell in a cascade before him that led to this tragedy?

A Monty Python skit on our subject would undoubtedly be called the "Dominoes of Peril" and those whacky English comedians from decades ago would have had a fun time pointing out what makes a task perilous. Peril means to "expose to danger," but if you go back to ancient Latin we find two origins. First, there is *experiri* = *to try;* as when we experiment at something. So that's where some of the *per-* comes from. The second Latin origin is *periculum* = *danger.* Put it all together and we learn from the ancients in togas and from silly Brits that the systems dominoes we speak of, these "Dominoes of Peril," put our workers in a position *to try danger.*

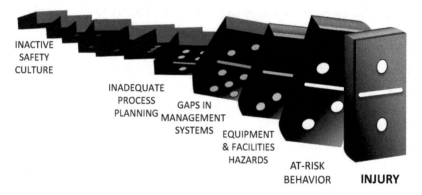

For the young South African, the initial design of the crushing machine and its lack of maintenance accessibility was a domino perfectly lined up to cause the mechanic to try danger by climbing on top of the active machine; the lack of plumbing lined up the debris perfectly to require him to try danger by using his arms to clear an opening.

Is it possible to mitigate all the environmental or system hazards at a worksite? Efforts to engineer guards, protective equipment, and barriers take a big bite out of injury rates. Constantly changing people, processes, tools and equipment conspire with aging employees, processes, tools and equipment to keep hazard mitigation a moving target. In this young mechanic's case, fixed ladders on the processing unit and view windows had long fallen into disrepair. The dominos had fallen into perfect places for an injury to occur.

Management decisions, especially decisions made without considering the safety implications, can fail to remove perilous dominoes or worse, put new a new domino perfectly in place. Well-documented manage-ment-level decisions favoring production over safety stand out when major disasters such as the Deepwater Horizon and Big Branch Mine are investigated. However, we must realize that managers are humans too and act under the same behavioral principles as their workers. Most management decisions are well meaning yet at times create "systems failure creep" — hidden hazards and risks that no one knows about until physics and chemistry combine to harm someone.

The young mechanic had been asked the fix the oil leak because it was a maintenance day when his side of the mill was down for numerous repairs. Shutting down the mill for repairs is a well-meaning management decision to reduce equipment failure at the expense of production and safety. However, those same managers realize that every hour part of the mill is down will cost them substantial revenue in lost productivity. In the name of efficiency they split the maintenance team across the tasks to be done, so they could be done more quickly. Everyone had been told to "be safe." All the dominoes were set up precisely to create an exposure where this young man alone was doing a task that should be approached by a small team of mechanics. A team could provide the necessary support to find the leaks without putting an individual in peril.

Let's follow our own advice and not blame managers and label them as ignorant, greedy or blind to the impact of their own decisions. As I said, managers are humans and subject to the same principles of human behavior as workers. They too are part of the system perfectly designed to have them knowingly or unknowingly make decisions that result in peril. Like our workers, we assume managers constantly and consistently seek to make safe decisions. A manager isn't hired to hurt anyone. There are just barriers that keep managers from acting on the value they put toward safety. This topic deserves an entire book for itself!

To give credit where credit is due, managers constantly and consistently attempt to put systems in place that target worker behavior to promote safe work. These preventive, pro-safety systems attempt to "remove the dominoes" that could line up and cascade into at-risk behavior and injury.

If risk-taking is caused by a lack of competence in how to safely work around hazards, managers insert systems such as training to tackle the competence deficit. When the allure of risk-taking is too P^3 (prompt, probable and personal), managers intervene with discipline procedures and rewards and recognition schemes. When managers fear there are undiscovered, hidden hazards out there, they install inspection, audit, and other reporting systems to encourage folks to go out and find the exposures. When hazards are uncovered by reporting — or by the harm caused by serious incidents — managers engage systems that offer different ways of communicating instructions and expectations to mitigate the hazards. We execute lock-out-tag-out (LOTO), job safety analyses, pre-shift toolbox talks, standard operating procedures, incident analyses, monthly safety meetings, mentoring, certifications, permitting, and hold meetings upon meetings upon meetings amongst ourselves to make it all safer. Managers, give yourself a hearty pat on the back.

Pull the Domino

We want to find the dominoes that have been perfectly and perilously lined up to cause risk and injury. And when we discover the peril we want to pull that domino out to stop the eventual cascade. We want to find the hazard and mitigate it. We want to discover the deficit and correct it. We desperately want to find that perilous line of dominoes and break the chain.

Too often we wait until an injury occurs to do the proper analysis to identify deficits in facilities, equipment, or management systems that contributed to the risk. We're reactive. Too many safety practices are reactive. We find out too late and too often fail to discover the dangerous dominoes. Why? Because we are blinded to the real truth by blame.

So how do you identify the perilous dominoes so you can pull them proactively? It's really quite simple, you're doing it in your rehab: conduct your behavioral observations without attribution, discover risk.... then... just ask. Ask the redheaded woman at the auto manufacturing plant. Ask the supervisor teaching Green Hats how to take shortcuts. Ask the CAVEmen. Ask Sam who built himself his own guard. Ask Patricia who disabled her guard. Ask the heart-blessers concerned about Doris' daughter. Ask the earthworks employee who left his gloves on the ground. Ask Brenda who B-Hacks her behavior by arranging her PPE at the end of every shift. Remember these stories from past chapters? Ask any of the thousands of workers I've had the honor of meeting over the years. They are wise... they are your crystal ball.

It starts with Culture, your Crystal Ball

Remember, my definition of safety culture is "talking about safety." Talk to your workers; engage in systems that have them talk to each other and to you. And LISTEN!

Some safety culture surveys designed to measure employee perceptions of management systems can help. One such survey that my university lab helped validate asks employees and managers where potential dominoes are lined up for peril because of limitations in their safety management systems. Such surveys ask questions about key system issues such as work pressure, incident reporting, communication, training, discipline, and rewards and recognition. The survey should also ask questions about how manager and employee behaviors enhance interpersonal support for safety. Survey results then help managers know where their efforts are most needed to do their part in pulling out the dangerous dominoes.

Frankly I find surveys too sterile to get at the raw specific reasons why people take risks. Surveys are fraught with bias, misinterpretations, and misrepresentations. They may be a good starting point, they can open eyes and ears, but there is no substitute for talking and listening.

Conversations can be messy at first. When I speak to employees about cascading dangerous dominoes I elicit different responses. Sometimes animated workers start complaining how safety incidents are mostly management's fault because "they" have "failed" to provide safe equipment and facilities; or "they" push production and budget over safety; or "they" rely on the workers to do all on the job training with folks who are too green to know better; or "they" blame workers through the discipline program, or…or…or… the complaint typically points at some mysterious manager named "they."

I always retort, "Well then 'they' should be fired! Wait. Who are 'they'?" No one ever knows, because these systems are complex. We've made this point before. Because of this complexity it's too easy for managers to blame the worker. This same complexity also makes it too easy for workers to blame the managers, the nebulous "they." In bad safety cultures you hear the word "they" and "them" a lot.

I learned in elementary school that when you point a finger at someone who you think is at fault, you have the rest of your fingers pointing back at you. Who is the first person you need to look to in order to improve this system to reduce injuries? The first person should be you.

"They" is the poison word lurking behind the blaming and other dysfunctions that kill your safety culture. "WE" is the antidote to fix it.

Imagine an empowered workforce and management working together as a "WE" to constantly search for dominoes to pull <u>before</u> peril sets in. That's how a culture reduces injuries.

A discovered domino can keep us from taking a risk (trying danger). When the discovered fault in the system gets fixed, a domino is pulled and the cascade toward injury is thwarted. When workers team up to help out the older guy (like me) to choose the tasks that his body is still able to do without strain, a domino is pulled. When a manager looks at the time and budget estimates for the job bid and works with the planner to consider the potential fatigue of her workers, a domino gets pulled. When a railroad dispatcher using his radio calls to ask engineers where they ran into uneven tracks so maintenance can add them to the inspection list, a domino gets pulled.

INACTIVE
SAFETY
CULTURE

INADEQUATE
PROCESS ~~GAPS IN~~
PLANNING ~~MANAGEMENT~~
~~SYSTEMS~~ EQUIPMENT
& FACILITIES
HAZARDS   AT-RISK
BEHAVIOR   **INJURY**

All these pulled dominoes keep some individual, somewhere, safe…
often someone the domino-puller doesn't even know. Finding and
pulling the perilous dominoes saves employees from putting themselves at-risk, either knowingly or unknowingly.

Target the Domino to Pull

How do we know which domino to pull? In complex work environments we certainly are not working with the limited 28 domino
tiles kids get out of a standard domino box. Your work environment
probably resembles some of the domino arrays that you can find
on YouTube, where the chain of domino tiles spans an entire room
spreading into multiple chains and looping back again, raising up levels
and coming down ledges. All these dominoes conspire to put a worker
in the perfect position to take a risk. You have a myriad of known and
unknown hazards, environmental conditions, tools in varying degrees
of disrepair, aging and changing equipment, volatile chemicals, melted

stuff, frozen stuff, brand new Green Hat employees, weather, old farts, new processes without operating procedures, old processes with out-of-date procedures, contractors without a clue, production quotas, labor issues, great trainers who quit the company, deer season, flavor of the month consultants, vendors who no longer support your lines, the new boss, plant upsets… need I go on?

Seems like a lot to manage, right? Consider the cascade of dominoes. No matter how large, all you have to do is take out the right domino and the cascade, the ripple effect, ends there. Before the injury. We need to target that domino — or, when we get good at targeting, we may find multiple dominoes to pull.

How do we go about targeting the right domino? By now, you should know:

1) **Observe behaviors neutrally to find the risks;**

2) **Ask your workers why the risks are taken, and add the critical third step;**

3) **Apply the science to understand the cause of behavior.**

Remember, each worker arrives at a decision point. Sometimes we have the opportunity to make a conscious decision. Most times decisions happen far from our consciousness, where decisions are made automatically based on our learning history. We then construct our reasoning after the fact. When we have more experience with the outcomes of these decisions, we develop rules that we apply to ourselves afterward to explain our discriminations. These rules we tell ourselves state the causal relationships we experience over time:

"In <u>this</u> situation…
If I act <u>this way</u> …
Then <u>this</u> will happen."

Seen this sentence before? If not go back and read the previous chapter where we learned that antecedents (*in this situation*) precede behavior with the context that directs the behavior... kind of like telling the worker "*now's a good time to do the behavior.*" Consequences (*Then this will happen*) are the outcome of the behavior that can reinforce behavior (increase the probability) or punish behavior (decrease the probability).

If we are aware of the behaviors that put our workers at-risk (*if I act this way*) then we can analyze the real and potential antecedents and consequences to target the domino we need to find. But our complacency to take the path of least resistance, not do a thorough analysis, and instead come up with the fastest, simplest answer can get in the way.

Too often our antecedents are contrived and we make the misguided assumption that they motivate the worker to work safe. "Awareness session" variations, including training, aim to motivate behavior. They don't. Workers may "feel" motivated; they may "intend" to do the right thing. But when they go back to work they find themselves in the same situation again. Nothing has really changed, nor will their behavior over the long term.

When we think we are training, in many cases we are really just educating. While education makes the intellectual case for engaging in safe behaviors, the educated don't actually come in contact with any meaningful practice and feedback needed to change behavior.

Think about it... would you rather have sex education.... Or sex training. I believe the later would be more motivating.

Classroom and online virtual training are not nearly as effective as on-the-job (OTJ) training. Now there are many potential problems with OTJ training including normalization of deviance. Still, OTJ has a distinct advantage over classrooms, physical or virtual. Whereas classrooms are all antecedent-based processes, OTJ allows the learner to engage in the task in context and experience a consequence. Here the mentor not only instructs but gives direct immediate feedback after the trainee performs the behavior. The mentor shapes behavior to become fluent and effective and safe and does not stop until this happens. If the behavior is not fluent (reliably happening all the time, quickly, with little cognitive load) then behaviors will drift and vary. Unfortunately most training programs end up in drift because they do not become fluent.

Similarly, we can also contrive our consequences. We contrive reward, incentive, and recognition programs. We have finally figured out that providing an incentive for reaching a goal of so many safe days only punishes reporting injuries, leaving us more blind and unsafe than we were prior to the goal. I've seen incentive programs for behavioral safety programs that were perfectly designed to achieve pencil whipping. All those raffles, pizza parties, and company-monogrammed swag (I have a collection!) might make people feel good, but they don't change behavior.

We also contrive discipline programs. An antecedent isn't effective without being associated with consequence. Rules are ineffective without a consequence. Typically, the consequence associated with rules is some type of discipline.

Consider the law connected to the "55 MPH" signs on the highway associated with speeding tickets. Even with the law and associated discipline, our traffic police have to enhance the P^3 of the tickets by being visible on the side of the road, pointing radar at oncoming cars, rigging fixed cameras and radar, and giving feedback to motorists with those electronic signs telling us our speed. Yet, according to the U.S. National Highway Traffic Safety Administration, 70 percent of Americans report in surveys that they speed some of the time; 30 percent of these say the speed all the time AND this all shows that behavior has little to do with attitudes; the overwhelming majority of survey respondents (91 percent) agreed with the statement, "*Everyone should obey the speed limits because it is the law.*"

Contrived antecedents and consequences can work but they often don't pass the P^3 test and fail to help the worker discriminate the right behavior at the right time for the right reasons. We will just be left with empty exhortations. And, trust me, the natural, non-contrived world will direct and motivate the worker to take risks.

Instead, the most effective antecedents and consequences are naturally occurring and indigenous to the environment where the work is being done. They naturally occur, help the worker discriminate their actions to the point of fluency, and pass the P^3 test. Consider asking these questions to your workforce as you continue your rehab:

A. Ask how training, tool availability, equipment flaws, perceived time pressure, unreported hazards and near misses, supervision, and work flow leave the worker in the position to take a risk. Find out the real-world antecedents that direct at-risk behavior or fail to direct safe behavior.

B. Ask about workers' past experience doing the task. Was the safe way to do the task cumbersome or ineffective? Did they adopt a risk in an effort to save time or trouble? What can be changed in the task to alleviate the "costs" of the safe alternatives? Seek to find out the real-world consequences that reinforce at-risk behavior or punish safe behavior.

The Most Important Domino

Since I was a child I've always been fascinated with the physics of cascading dominoes, where a five-millimeter high domino can eventually topple the Empire State building in a 29-domino string (you can see a demonstration of this on YouTube). Similarly, the smallest behavior can start (or stop) the cascade that could avert catastrophe. This is a lesson for those of us trying to impact process safety as well. If someone would have simply replaced the battery in the blowout preventers prior to deployment, the Deepwater Horizon would not have been destroyed.

I know this new domino theory is complex because of the plethora of system realities that can cause an at-risk behavior. We have an ace in the hole.

Consider the very first domino at the beginning of the potentially cascading chain perilously leading to risk and injury. What is the first domino, the one, if pulled, that could protect the worker even if the rest of the dominoes are perfectly set up for failure? Perhaps it's only five-millimeters big in contrast to the long cascade of other system factors.

In the midst of all the hazards,
in the midst of faulty tools or equipment and processes,
in the midst of untrained tasks, confusing instructions, and unaware supervisors,

> you find your fellow workers.

Fellow workers know where the hazards are. Fellow workers know the risks being taken. Fellow workers are aware of the changes being made around them. Fellow workers are more likely to have influence to change behavior.

Will that first domino stay in place with complacent or fearful workers who fail to stop and coach their peers when risks are being taken? Will that first domino stay in place when a worker fails to alert their peers by reporting close calls, minor injuries, and hazards? Will that domino stay in place when workers teach each other how to take short cuts? This first domino represents an inactive safety culture, a culture where no one is talking and if they are talking, it's the CAVEmen complaining or the supervisor teaching Green Hats how to take short cuts.

Fortunately, here is the secret ingredient: fellow workers care.

Your fellow workers can pull the very first domino. An active safety culture, cultivated by the workers, has the most power to stop a perilous chain of events in its track before someone gets injured. If the culture has been built around actively caring, where fellow workers recognize risk and are willing and able to coach their peers to avoid risk, then we can pull the first domino out before the cascade causes harm.

The final question to target the first domino:

C. Take a close look at your safety culture. Are your workers taught how to take risks by others? Is risk-taking reinforced socially by fellow workers or even management? Alternatively (here is the big one), would a peer be likely to stop and coach a fellow worker if they saw the risky behavior occurring?

In our young mechanic's case the task, equipment, staffing, and even supervision put him in a position to take the risk he did. What if there had been fellow workers aware of the hazardous tasks occurring around them? What if just one of them would have checked up on the young man, alerting him on the risks he was taking, instructing him in the safe alternatives, lending additional hands, helping him problem-solve to reduce the hazard, or being willing to help him stop the job and speak to management? What if that first domino was pulled? Our mechanic would still have his arm... and his job.

One of my clients is a railroad here in the United States. One of their service units (in Texas) has a very strong behavioral safety program that has built a strong culture of talking. This team adopted a "Pull the Domino" program where team members hand dominoes to employees, managers, contractors or anyone (I got one!) to thank them for creating better ways to work safe, give a helping hand, or stop a line when there is a problem. The team recognizes that when one domino falls, they all fall. "Pulling the Domino" refers to stopping that cycle; it means that they vow to remove any "domino pieces" before they cascade into a problem. WE solve the problem, WE keep people safe.

In addition to cascading dominoes, back in Texas when the adults were not playing Texas 42 we kids were fond of stacking the dominoes into fortresses. The idea was to build a fortress strong enough to withstand the impact of a sliding domino slung at the structure by your opponent.

Perhaps that's a great metaphor for how a safety culture protects its people. A culture where people talk to other people to solve problems is able to pull dominoes out of the cascading lineup. These pulled dominoes transform into solutions that protect workers. These solutions can now be stacked in a fortress that forms a united front representing trust and determination to withstand hazards and risk. You can see this fortress grow and strengthen as the culture builds. It's an amazing thing.

~~DYS~~FUNCTIONAL PRACTICE: PULL THE DOMINO

Your system is perfectly designed to get the results you received because your system is perfectly designed to produce the behaviors you shaped. Most errors are associated with human behavior — BUT 94 percent of human behavior is due to the system that caused it.

Human behavior is not the cause of injuries; at-risk behavior results from other factors, such as the design of machinery, the layout of work space, inaccessibility of tools and PPE, decisions to rush production, and so on.

Target the right part of your system to change. Observe behaviors to find risks. Then ask your workers why the risks are taken. Analyze the antecedents (e.g., training, tool availability, instructions, time pressure) that direct at-risk behavior or fail to direct safe behavior. Then identify the consequences that reinforce at-risk behavior or punish safe behavior to save time or trouble.

An operational definition of safety culture is "people talking about safety." Talk to your workers and LISTEN! Engage in systems that have them talk to each other. Peers who coach peers are the first line of defense... and the most effective behavior change strategy.

POSTSCRIPT:
My Job as a Labeler

THE FIELD OF BEHAVIOR SCIENCE HAS AN IMPACT FAR beyond workplace safety. Its principles have been applied with great success to increase learning and decrease bullying in our schools; help shape policy in governments; increase performance and decrease concussions in sports; build trust in community policing; address patient safety concerns in hospitals; train animals to do cool things like hunt for bombs; reduce sexually transmitted diseases; increase health across the spectrum, especially among sedentary long-haul truck drivers — the list goes on and on. If there is a human (or animal) there are behaviors. Where there are behaviors, there is the opportunity to make a positive impact. Go to Behavior.org and learn all the areas that may touch your life and see what we're trying to do sharing behavior science.

One of the biggest success areas for behavior science (besides behavioral safety) is its application to human services. Applied behavior analysis (ABA) is the single biggest empirically-validated approach for treating autism through skills training and parental coaching. We've been able to address all sorts of human challenges to mental and physical abilities.

Earlier in my career I worked with severely mentally disabled individuals. Some of the nicest people you'll ever meet. I was working my way through graduate school and landed this part-time contract job as a staff psychologist. I was working with a group of about 15 folks with severe mental disabilities and other challenges, so much so that many couldn't live life on their own. Their biological parents could not adequately care for them. They were wards of the state. They lived together in their residence where the professional staff fed them, cleaned them, groomed them and provided what training and social life they could. We all loved working with these 15 folks and considered the residence their home; we were their guests.

My job was to come in once a week for a couple hours, interact with the residents and create programs to try to shape basic life and social behaviors I also conducted assessments such as intelligence tests. These were not standard intelligence tests administered to "normal" folks like you or I (granted, the word "normal" may be a stretch for my readers and I). These intelligence tests assessed very low cognitive ability. There were no question and answer sections; many of these folks could not use language. Instead, I was assessing if they could groom themselves, use a fork, respond to instructions and the like.

One of the residents was Violet. Violet was a woman in her 40s with a hunched back and mean scowl on her face at all times. She was a cranky soul who would, on occasion, sling her plates on the floor or against small doors.

Back then we used the label "mentally retarded" although now the clinical term is "intellectual disability". Regardless, this was the clinical label back then and Violet fell squarely into that category. I conducted the special intelligence test on her and her IQ was around 15 (for reference, average IQ is 100). This put her in the "profoundly mentally retarded" classification. In particular, her verbal abilities were strikingly limited, typically reduced to sounds resembling simple words.

Unfortunately, events came to a point where Violet got particularly agitated and slammed her fist through a sheet rock wall. We knew incidents like these were inevitable with Violet because she would slap her right arm against her left shoulder when she'd start getting more and more agitated. This time the outburst was too much. We knew something had to be done. She could have hurt herself or others.

I was part of a team that served these special people like Violet. In addition to me, the psychologist, we had a psychiatrist who administered medications. Many of the residents were on some kind of psychotropic medication for the additional psychological disorders that unfortunately came with their genetic maladies. In addition to the staff we also had on the team a social worker as a director, a new guy named Bob. He was a funny, goofy guy. One of the wisest people I've ever met.

We had a team meeting. Bob first asked the psychiatrist for his opinion of what could be done for Violet. The psychiatrist said he was treating her for hallucinations. He had diagnosed her as "schizophrenic," a psychological disorder accompanied by hallucinations, delusions, and disorganized thinking. The staff reported that Violet often hallucinated that an evil pony rode on her left shoulder. Evidently, the theory was she was hitting herself on the shoulder to knock off the pony. Her left shoulder had deep bruises from the abuse.

For these hallucinations, Violet was on Haldol, a drug given to schizophrenics. It's a strong tranquilizer. If you take it, believe me, you'll not only reduce your daydreams but also just about all other cognitive activity. Violet was already on a pretty high dose. In the wake of the incident the psychiatrist recommended tripling the dose. That's a lot of chemicals to flood a brain.

Bob then asked my opinion. I described a number of behavioral programs I designed trying to shape behaviors to counter her violent, self-injurious behavior. We had a long discussion about the precursors to her behavior and the behavioral steps the staff should take to reduce the likelihood of violent outbursts. The staff contributed even more suggestions in what I thought was a fruitful team discussion.

But Bob was quiet and after listening to all our input he said, "*Hold on. Before we do chemical or behavioral interventions, let's consider physical solutions first.*" He wanted to learn what was going with Violet as a person, not some psychiatric or behavioral label. Bob was the director of the residence so his was the final decision.

Bob took Violet to get a physical, her first in many years. The attending physician noted a large bulge above her left foot and, through an X-ray, located a metal screw in her ankle. All of us had somehow missed this. Violet's body was deformed with a humpback and other contortions. So the large bulge around her ankle must have been considered just another deformity.

In reality, Violet had broken her ankle badly in her youth and surgeons put in the metal screw for healing. Her caregivers back then must have forgotten to have it taken out. Violet wasn't verbal, she couldn't tell anybody. In fact, she probably had no idea of any screw being there. Violet was probably 40 when the physician did the X-ray, perhaps 20 years after the screw was inserted. All she experienced was pain due to the calcification and swelling around the screw that had been in her ankle for decades.

Violet was in agony. Take all your old person aches and pains and multiply it exponentially. She couldn't understand what was happening, she couldn't tell anyone about how she felt, and her self-injurious behavior was her reaction to her agony. The pain was on her left side, pounding her left shoulder could have helped relieve some of the agony or perhaps it was an attempt to communicate. Trapped in pain, she released some of her aggravation in her increasingly violent behaviors.

Bob sent Violet to surgery to have the screw removed and the calcium deposits shaved away. She then spent a number of weeks undergoing physical therapy.

When Violet returned to the residence she was a different woman. She did not exhibit the violent behaviors; she was no longer "violent." She no longer was smacking the left side of her body, she was not "self-injurious." Soon Violet went off the Haldol completely and the staff reported no supposed hallucinations; she was no longer "schizophrenic." She was never any of these labels; she had been in pain, terrible pain. She wasn't in pain anymore.

Much to my amazement Violet started using more complex words upon her return to the residence! Previously I had administered my intelligence test on her and assigned her a clinical label of "profoundly mentally retarded." Now, with the pain gone, she started using the words she had always been capable of. She could name eating utensils, ask for access to the TV by name, and even call staff members by their names! She started grooming herself, eating without assistance and interacting with other residents and staff persons. She even lost the permanent scowl on her face and… smiled.

I did a new intelligence test and her IQ (a measure that is supposed to stay stable over your lifetime) jumped more than 15 points (a standard deviation!) with this new verbal and self-management behavior. But those behaviors were not "new." *All those skills were always there. We had failed to remove the barriers that kept her away from being her best.* The more skilled Violet had always been present, yet she was trapped by her pain and depending on us to get her out. Unfortunately we were busy assigning our labels instead of finding the root cause of her behaviors. Fortunately, Bob was wiser than us "doctors."

Bob (the wise man) wasn't done yet. He discovered Violet had cataracts. She couldn't see. After cataract surgery she came back smiling more, interacting more, and being more independent. She became downright huggy. She had turned into… shall we say … an "affectionate" person.

I left the job soon thereafter but I still remember my last day vividly. Violet, yes "Violent," came up and hugged me. She wouldn't let me go. And with that farewell, she used a full sentence, verbs and all: *Good bye, I will miss you….Tim.* She had used my name at the end, something that I thought she was too "retarded" to do. It was evident that even my new IQ label was inaccurate and too low. I was in tears as I drove away.

My job had been to help her. I was paid to help her. Trained to help her. I almost had my doctorate after nine years of college. The psychiatrist had an MD after even more education. The social worker, Bob, didn't have all this schooling or fancy degrees. But who among the "smart" people was the one who really saw Violet as she was, a whole person, not a label? It was the person who was with her every day. It was Bob who said we're not going to label. Instead, we're going to look at her world and understand why she is doing what she is doing. I often look back and thank Violet and Bob for this important lesson in my life.

Labeling is Counterproductive ... Get it Yet?

An important lesson learned conveyed throughout this book is that labeling is counterproductive for our safe work environments. We need to be a wise woman or man (like Bob) and understand what is going on in our workers' world and do something about that — instead of trying to do something about them. We change their environment, and by changing the environment, we change behavior.

Do workers need different, more available tools to work safe? Better, more behavioral training? Procedures that lessen fatigue? Supervision that doesn't encourage short cuts? Etcetera ... Etcetera. It's your job to be "Bob" and to do the analysis to find the causes of behaviors that put your workers at risk. It's your job to ensure your workers don't find themselves in a position of having to take those risks any longer.

> Understand what is going on in your workers' world and do something about that... instead of trying to do something about them. We change their environment, and by changing the environment, we change behavior.

We don't need to label. That won't get the job done.

Folks, dig deeper. Labels are artificial and superficial. Labels are an illusion. There's always a reason for the behavior that we get. We can all overcome our labels!

A Celebration is in Order!

When I was teaching a junior youth Sunday school class at my church I interacted with a wonderful group of young people. In my class was a young lady born with Downs Syndrome. An IQ test would have labeled her with an intellectual disability. Miranda was also one of the sweetest kids I associated with, but I knew she had a limited educational future, probably performing at a 6th grade level the rest of her life. She was 12 at the time. Every time we saw each other at church or in town I was always greeted with a big hug.

Six years later I got word that my university was extending its disability services to include intellectual disabilities. Most universities require professors to make accommodations for students with disabilities in much the same way institutions provide ramps and the like for students and staff with physical disabilities. Typically, I have students with learning disabilities like dyslexia or attention deficit disorder (ADD) who get extra time on exams and other accommodations so they can perform up to their intellectual abilities less encumbered by their disability. I'm happy to provide these accommodations so my students can perform to their potential.

The new message from my university was intellectual disabilities (previously called mental retardation) would be considered a classification for disability services. The administration also noted that students classified with mental retardation would be admitted into the student body to pursue degrees.

I was skeptical about allowing individuals with intellectual disabilities into the university system because their intellectual capabilities would not allow for the necessary learning to take place. Why should we set them up to fail to live up to the academic standards of our courses — regardless of any accommodations we provided them.

I am proud to have attended my Sunday school student Miranda's university graduation in my fancy doctoral robes indicating my learned status. I watched Miranda walk the stage to our cheers, pride on her face — a pride coming from hard work, much harder than those around her, facilitated by colleagues at my university much wiser than me. People willing to look beyond the label and create an environment for Miranda to succeed.

I stood with thousands attending as we joined in an ovation honoring a young lady whose life will deliver even more amazing feats. Once again I was humbled by the potential of human performance.

About the Author

Timothy Ludwig earned his Ph.D. at Virginia Tech researching the benefits of employee-driven behavioral safety programs under E. Scott Geller, and continuing his post-doctoral work in industrial engineering studying applications of W. Edwards Deming to quality and safety improvement. After graduation, Dr. Ludwig consulted with the Department of Energy to study and improve their management systems on the New Production Reactor project, a modern day Manhattan Project to build the next generation of tritium bomb. Thankfully the cold war ended and Dr. Ludwig proceeded to work with the U.S. Navy's acquisition community (NAVSEA, SPAWAR) engaging in strategic planning and process improvement. During his early career, Dr. Ludwig consulted with other government agencies, hospitals, industries, and distribution on quality improvement initiatives.

Tim's father was a preacher as well as a college professor and his mother was an elementary school teacher. So it's easy to understand why he wanted to be a teacher as well, and he has done so for more than 25 years. One of his favorite activities is presenting keynotes, where his teaching skills can deliver meaningful messages to educate and inspire. To this end, Dr. Ludwig has delivered more than 100 keynote speeches internationally. In his "day job" Dr. Ludwig is a Distinguished Graduate Professor at Appalachian State University, teaching in the nationally-recognized Industrial/Organizational Psychology and Human Resources Management Masters program. Dr. Ludwig's teaching has been recognized with the North Carolina University Board of Governors' Excellence Award and has been inducted into his University's Academy of Outstanding Teachers.

Dr. Ludwig founded and directs the Appalachian Safety Summit, bringing internationally-renowned behavioral safety experts to Appalachian State and allowing safety professionals to engage with these individuals in an intimate mountain setting.

Dr. Ludwig loves to write when he needs to get ideas out of his head; he does this through his website, books, magazine articles, blogs, and scholarly articles about his research. His popular website Safety-doc.com is a content-rich resource of safety culture stories, blogs, research, videos, and services. Dr. Ludwig was cited for the second time in Industrial Safety and Hygiene News (ISHN) "50 Leaders for Today and Tomorrow." Dr. Ludwig is the author of dozens of scholarly articles that empirically document the successes of methods to improve safety and quality in industry through behavior-based solutions. His books include *Intervening to Improve the Safety of Occupational Driving; Behavioral Systems: Understanding Complexity in Organizations; Behavioral Science Approaches to Process Safety: A Response to Industry's Call;* and *Dysfunctional Practices that Kill your Safety Culture.*

Dr. Ludwig served as Editor of the *Journal of Organizational Behavior Management,* the source of the seminal research on behavioral safety published in the 1970s. The *Journal* still often publishes current peer-reviewed behavioral safety research. Dr. Ludwig is the past President of the Organizational Behavior Management Network that boasts the top behavioral scientists who apply their craft to organizational challenges, including safety. Dr. Ludwig is invited to present his research and behavioral models at numerous scholarly conferences internationally.

Dr. Timothy Ludwig endeavors to use his science and practice to have an impact on the welfare of the human race. Dr. Ludwig serves on the Board of the Cambridge Center for Behavioral Studies whose mission to advance the scientific study of behavior and its humane application to the solution of practical problems, including the prevention and relief of human suffering. Dr. Ludwig serves on the Cambridge Center's Commission for the Accreditation of Behavioral Safety Programs that seeks to recognize and share the best practices of the very top performing behavioral safety programs in the world. Currently there are 23 accredited companies worldwide. This wealth of information can be accessed for free by safety professionals seeking to improve their behavioral safety programs by going to Behavior.org and chosing the Safety topic area. The CCBS Commission also co-hosts the annual national conference Behavioral Safety Now to disseminate best practices, current scientific findings, and practical advice to more than 400 professionals a year.

Dr. Ludwig has more than 30 years of experience in research and practice in behavioral safety. He integrates empirical findings into his safety consulting. Dr. Ludwig has been around the world in his consulting practice helping assess, design, and implement safety and quality improvement programs worldwide. He also has provided his expertise in Behavior Systems Analysis, Strategic Planning, and Quality Improvement to numerous private and government organizations.

Tim lives in the beautiful and ancient mountains of North Carolina with his wife Dr. Lori Ludwig, dog and cat. His three children are beginning their adult lives as they move on to college, bachelors' degrees, and beyond.

CPSIA information can be obtained
at www.ICGtesting.com
Printed in the USA
LVHW051719010420
651874LV00006B/1580